1986

READING
FICTION

P9-ASN-785

Stephen Minot

Prentice-Hall, Inc.,
Englewood Cliffs, New Jersey 07632

Library of Congress Cataloging in Publication Data

Minot, Stephen.
   Reading fiction.

   Includes index.
   1. Fiction—Technique. I. Title.
PN3355.M56 1985   808.3   84-13319
ISBN 0-13-754995-4

Editorial/production supervision and
   interior design: Virginia McCarthy
Cover design: Ben Santora
Manufacturing buyer: Harry P. Baisley

The Soujourner from *The Ballad of the Sad Cafe and Collected Short Stories* by Carson McCullers. Copyright © 1955 by Carson McCullers. Reprinted by permission of Houghton Mifflin Company.

On the Road reprinted by permission of Harold Ober Associates Incorporated. Copyright © 1934, 1962 by Langston Hughes.

A & P copyright © 1962 by John Updike. Reprinted from *Pigeon Feathers and Other Stories*, by John Updike, by permission of Alfred A. Knopf, Inc.

Excerpt from *Maude Martha* from *The World of Gwendolyn Brooks* by Gwendolyn Brooks. Copyright, 1953, by Gwendolyn Brooks Blakely. Reprinted by permission of Harper & Row, Publishers, Inc.

Excerpt from *The Sun Also Rises* copyright 1926 Charles Scribner's Sons; copyright renewed 1954 Ernest Hemingway. Reprinted with the permission of Charles Scribner's Sons.

Printed in the United States of America

10 9 8 7 6 5 4 3 2 1

ISBN 01 0-13-754995-4

Prentice-Hall International, Inc., *London*
Prentice-Hall of Austrlia Pty. Limited, *Sydney*
Editora Prentice-Hall do Brasil, Ltda., *Rio de Janeiro*
Prentice-Hall Canada Inc., *Toronto*
Prentice-Hall of India Private Limited, *New Delhi*
Prentice-Hall of Japan, Inc., *Tokyo*
Prentice-Hall of Southeast Asia Pte. Ltd., *Singapore*
Whitehall Books Limited, *Wellington, New Zealand*

CONTENTS

Once again . . . for Ginny.

PREFACE
FOR STUDENTS

This preface is important and brief. It describes five specific ways to make full use of *Reading Fiction*.

First, if you own your own copy, mark it up. Carefully underline what you think is important and add marginal notations to sections you may wish to review. Studies have shown that students who take notes or mark their own books recall more than those who don't—even if they never look at the notations again. The very process of selective underlining and note taking helps to imprint the material in your mind.

Second, pay particular attention to the terms in italics. You will find them useful when discussing fiction in class because they will help to keep your analysis precise. For the same reason they will also be invaluable when you are writing papers about literature. In addition, they have a long-range benefit: The concepts they describe will help you to see more and enjoy more in good fiction years after you have stopped taking courses.

Third, apply these concepts to stories and novels you have read or are presently reading. For example, when you come to the distinctions between *flat* and *round* characters, stop for a moment and see if you can use these terms to describe the characters in some work of fiction not included in this volume. You may find that what you had previously considered a minor character actually serves some essential function in the development of the plot or theme. Or when you are introduced to the five *narrative modes* of fiction, examine a paragraph of any story or novel and analyze for yourself how each sentence or phrase comes under one of these headings. Then compare that sample with a passage by another writer to see how that balance shifts. New concepts will become far more meaningful and useful if you take the time to apply them to the fiction you are reading.

There are several good examples of fiction included in this volume which I use to illustrate a variety of literary concepts. But reading the analysis provided is only a first step to understanding. The next step is up to you. Take the time to apply the same sort of analysis to whatever other works of fiction you are reading. In short, don't go limp; be an active reader.

Fourth, use the glossary while you read this book. Whenever you come to an important term about which you are unsure, stop and consult the glossary. It gives a brief definition and a reference to where in this book the concept is described in detail. You will save time in the long run if you keep reviewing as you read.

Finally, if you are taking a course, make a conscious effort to use these terms and concepts in class discussions and even in casual conversation. There is no value in memorizing a term like *means of perception* or *limited omniscience* if you don't soon reach the point of using it naturally and easily. These terms haven't been introduced just to make you sound literary. They refer to concepts which will help you to get more out of fiction.

At first, it takes a little effort to use new terms accurately. The same is true of any new skill—from sports to music. But by using this critical vocabulary in conversation both in class and informally with friends, you will find that it soon becomes a natural and useful way of looking at literature. Once that happens, reading fiction will become a far richer experience for you.

PREFACE
FOR TEACHERS

One of our continuing problems in the teaching of fiction is that there is no longer a canon of literary works which all students have read. It is difficult to find a novel—much less a story—with which even half the members of one class are familiar.

This is not likely to change. But even though there is no agreement about which novels and stories should serve as the core of the English curriculum, we do share two closely related goals: showing students the difference between passive and active reading, and helping them to find pleasure in relatively sophisticated fiction.

Reading Fiction has been written with these two goals in mind. It does not prescribe any one way to teach, nor does it assume familiarity with any one set of authors. It should be of equal value in courses which focus on the short story and those which deal with the novel. The emphasis is on the art of reading itself—not just for speed, but for full understanding and, equally important, enjoyment.

I have kept this work concise with the hope that it will supplement, not dominate, the works of fiction you have assigned. Each chapter focuses on a specific aspect of fiction which must be understood if a reader is to appreciate a short story or novel fully. My approach is not historical but analytical and practical: How can one draw the most from the works assigned in a particular course? How can one increase the ability and the desire to read fiction in future years?

At the end of almost every chapter there is a section called "Topics for Analysis." These topics can be used in two different ways. If you ask your students to consider them carefully when reading the assignment, you will have a natural starting point for the next class discussion. The topics can also be used as the basis for theme assignments or examination questions. You may wish to revise some of them so that they apply directly to the fiction you have assigned. In this way, each chapter can be closely integrated with your own course offerings.

Reading Fiction also contains four short stories and excerpts from four novels to illustrate specific literary concepts. These should serve to keep the analysis from becoming abstract and detached from concrete examples. I hope, however, that you will encourage your students to apply these critical terms to the works of fiction which you have assigned in the course. Sometimes this requires a special effort, but it is essential if the terminology is to become a part of their active vocabulary. As soon as they feel at home with these concepts, they will be able to make far better use of whatever works are included in your syllabus. In addition, they will have acquired the tools with which to enjoy fiction in future years.

I am convinced that one of the keys to a successful class is active student participation. *Reading Fiction* should help encourage this by introducing those concepts which would otherwise have to be explained in class every year. With this in mind, I recommend that you assign this book at the beginning of the term and use it as a base for the analysis of whatever works of fiction have been selected for the course. Your students will soon share a common vocabulary with which to discuss any novel or story. This should increase the amount of class time you can devote to informal class discussion.

The order of the chapters is designed to match the organization of most fiction courses. Concepts such as *active* versus *passive* reading, *simple* versus *sophisticated* fiction, *characterization,* and *setting* are dealt with early so that they can be discussed and applied while the students are just beginning their first assignments in the fiction itself. More sophisticated aspects come later: *tone, style, symbolic suggestion.* The discussion of *theme* comes toward the end since students in a novel course need time to complete their first work before appraising its central concern.

Ideally the next-to-last chapter, "Writing about Fiction," should precede the due date of the first student paper. In courses requiring weekly themes, however, it might be helpful to assign this section earlier. I also hope that the final chapter, "Enjoying Fiction," will be emphasized. My goal, like that of most teachers, is to encourage students to go on reading sophisticated fiction for pleasure long after they have graduated. This chapter should help to make the end of any literature course the beginning of a lifelong interest.

chapter 1

FIRST IMPRESSIONS

simple versus sophisticated fiction
passive versus active reading
previewing a new work
the opening scene: who? where?
when? how? what?
practice in active reading

SIMPLE VERSUS
SOPHISTICATED FICTION

There is an enormous variety of fiction available and little agreement about what is "good." This is as it should be. Taste is a personal matter and every reader has different interests. There is one very helpful distinction, however, which is not a matter of taste. Some stories and novels are relatively *simple* and, at the other end of the scale, some are more *sophisticated*.

These terms are purely descriptive. They do not suggest that one type of writing is "good" and the other "bad." They are borrowed from biology where they are used to describe types of living matter. Creatures with one or two cells are relatively *simple*, while mammals, on the other hand, are more *sophisticated* forms of life. Between the two extremes, there are almost limitless gradations.

Simple fiction deals with characters who are one-dimensional, situations which are straightforward and often familiar, and themes which are frequently clichés ("Crime doesn't pay," "Good guys eventually win," "Money isn't everything"). Simple fiction is often (but not always) found in women's magazines and in "costume gothic" novels. It takes on a different form in the so-called flesh magazines. Many (but not all) of the novels on the best-seller list are in various degrees simple fiction. Their dramatic counterpart is seen nightly on commercial television. Fiction and drama on this level hold interest without requiring much effort and so serve a function. But they are very quickly forgotten. They do not make a lasting impression on us. They rarely broaden our horizons.

Sophisticated fiction, on the other hand, usually deals with characters who are both unique and complex, situations which have many ramifications, and themes which reveal subtle insights. Such works, also called *literary fiction,* are intricate not to confuse the reader but to provide a greater range of meaning and pleasure.

True, you may have to work harder to appreciate the subtleties of a sophisticated work of fiction, but often it will stay with you as if it were a part of your own life. The characters linger in your memory as if you had actually known them, the situation remains vivid as if you had lived through it. Such fiction extends your experience and expands your vision. For many, it's just more satisfying.

Both simple and sophisticated fiction have their functions, and enjoying one doesn't mean you have to reject the other. But it is a great mistake to confuse the two. If you begin to read a sophisticated story or novel with the expectation of instant reward, you may be disappointed at the outset. You will probably start skimming, missing what is there for you to enjoy. It would be like playing a taped symphony at twice the prescribed speed just so you can "get to the good part."

Learning to read sophisticated fiction is more complex than playing a tape at the correct speed, but it is within the grasp of anyone. And once learned, it becomes a skill and a source of pleasure which is never lost. This does not mean that you will or should give up reading simple fiction from time to time. Everyone enjoys "turning off" on occasion. But for lasting pleasure you will find yourself returning to the broader, richer experience found in more sophisticated work.

PASSIVE VERSUS ACTIVE READING

Much of our daily reading is essentially a passive act. We skim over the front page of the paper, the sports section, or a news magazine with our mind half on the words and half on other matters. Later, we may recall that there was a murder or an uprising somewhere or that a particular team won, but we wouldn't want to be quizzed on the details.

This is a natural reflection of the society in which we live. We are bombarded with print in a way never experienced in previous centuries, and we can't be bothered to read every news item and breakfast cereal box carefully. In addition, there is a certain escapist pleasure in light novels and stories which we read the way we listen to music in the supermarket. This "summer reading" has its place. But you will cheat yourself if you use the same approach with fiction which is literarily sophisticated.

Sophisticated fiction requires active reading. This doesn't mean you have to be grim about it and sit in an uncomfortable chair. But it does mean that you have to stay alert. Equally important, you have to know what to look for. Helping you to develop this ability is one of the goals of this book.

THE PREVIEW

To be an active reader of literary fiction you should start thinking about a new work even before turning to the first page. If you are familiar with the author, review in your own mind what else you have read by the same writer. What kinds of characters has this author worked with in the past? What settings? Was the style distinctive? This new work may be a departure in many ways; but if you begin by placing it in a context, you will be thinking analytically from the start. This is essential for active reading.

In many cases, of course, the author will be new to you. Even then it is worth making a careful note of the title. It is all too easy to finish a short story without recalling the title. When you do this, however, you run the risk of missing a central image or an important emphasis which should have been kept in mind from the very beginning.

In the case of novels, look over the organizational pattern. Are there chapters? Do they have titles which may serve as clues to the development of the work? Are the chapters grouped into "books," those larger units (often three) which sometimes signal a shift in time, in mood, or in point of view? If you know about these divisions in advance, you will be prepared for whatever function they may have.

THE OPENING SCENE

The first few pages of a short story and the first chapter of a novel are enormously important. Imagine that you are a stranger stepping into someone else's life and that you are being introduced to people you have never met before. Not only that, but you realize that certain events have occurred which you have to find out about through the conversation. It is up to you to listen carefully.

If you have been a regular viewer of television dramas, as most of us have, keep in mind how that form of entertainment may have shaped your attitude toward any form of story telling. We snap on the set, half listen to the commercials, and then passively stare at the opening scene. We expect to be entertained. That's what a "good" show is supposed to do. If that first scene is slow or confusing, we may start talking with a friend or read a magazine, waiting for "something to happen."

We all do this, encouraged by the scriptwriters themselves, whose job it is to capture the attention of the largest number of people as quickly as possible. The problem is that when we turn to sophisticated short stories and novels, we may bring with us that same child-like demand: Entertain me!

If a story or novel seems to begin slowly, resist the temptation to skim. In fact, you should read the first few pages of a story and the opening of a novel more slowly than any other section. Get everything straight right from the start. Then you can pick up the pace.

What should you be looking for during that initial period? It varies with every work, but there are five basic questions you should ask:

- Who's involved?
- Where are we?
- When is this?
- How is this being told?
- What's happening?

These are like the questions every reporter asks when taking notes on a news event. In a sense you *are* a reporter at the outset. It is important to get the facts rapidly and accurately before you move on to more subtle concerns.

Who's involved?

Every work of fiction is based on characters. They are usually introduced early. Try to get to know each new character as quickly as you can.

Names are important. If the book is your own, circle or underline each new name the first time it appears. This is more than just a matter of preparing for a quiz. If you slide over the names of characters early in a work, you may well become confused later and have to reread some of the opening scenes. This takes a lot of time and will spoil your pleasure as well.

When reading novels which have many characters, it is well worth taking the time to keep a list of the central ones with brief descriptions for each—no more than a phrase or two. This will actually increase your reading speed as well as your comprehension because there is a natural tendency to slow down when a character appears whose identity you can't quite place. And, of course, that list will be invaluable when it is time to review.

As soon as you have two or more characters interacting, the relationship will often tell you a lot. Whether you are dealing with a mother and daughter, two brothers, husband and wife, two friends, or even two strangers, notice whether that relationship is essentially harmonious or antagonistic, one of equality or inequality, relaxed or tense. Characters in fiction are rarely in isolation; they form a complex pattern of interrelationships.

Where are we?

The moment you begin a new story or novel, you are being transported to a new place. Start by determining the immediate setting: Are we inside or out? In someone's home or on a city street? In a court room or at a police station? Look for clues which will help to place you. As soon as possible, try to judge whether the setting is being used in a significant way. The next chapter is a story by Carson McCullers called "The Sojourner." You will have no difficulty identifying the setting as New York City and later as Paris, but notice carefully how references to many other countries at the very opening of that story help to identify the central character as a restless wanderer.

In addition to geographical place, consider the social setting. In Chapter 4 you will be reading "On the Road" by Langston Hughes. It deals with an unemployed black man during the Depression. You will see right away that both class and race are essential elements in that story. If you read the first paragraph of each story carefully, you will see that settings can be used in entirely different ways.

When is this?

Time is really another aspect of setting. The historical period is often what you will notice first. Characters living in, say, the Victorian era cannot be judged as if they were contemporary men and women in costume.

On a more subtle level, the season may be an important element. In one of the stories included in this volume, a great deal is made of the fact that the events take place in early spring. In another, winter takes on symbolic significance.

Time also refers to the age of the central character. How old you are radically affects your view of the world. Some stories deal with children, viewing the situation through their eyes; other works concern the adolescent years, the middle years, or old age. Each stage in a person's life embodies a different set of attitudes. In three of the four stories included in this volume, age is a highly significant factor.

How is this being told?

Almost all fiction is presented either in the *first person* or the *third person*. Here are these two approaches used to begin the same story:

(A)

It was March 31 and I had survived still another Maine winter. Now, my solitary lunch finished, I stood for a moment by the large living-room window and looked down over the white stubble of glazed brush to the sea.

(B)

It was March 31 and Isaac Bates had survived still another Maine winter. Now, his solitary lunch finished, he stood for a moment by the large living-room window and looked down over the white stubble of glazed brush to the sea.

In passage *A*, the first-person version, we can be sure that all the events of the story which follows are going to be presented through the narrator's eyes. We will see what he sees, know what he knows, and the thoughts we are given will be his. He may *guess* what others are thinking ("I decided my friend must really be angry"), but as readers we will depend on this character for everything we learn. Such a character is referred to as the *means of perception* since the material is presented from his or her *point of view*. This is the subject of Chapter 7.

In the case of the third-person version, passage *B*, there are more possibilities. Of course, the entire story may come to us through that same character, just as it did when the first person was used. But if a second character were added to that opening scene, he or she might serve as the means of perception instead. It might read like this:

(C)

Seth, standing there in silence, watched his old friend, Isaac, light a cigar and stare out the window. How, he wondered, could anyone enjoy such a desolate view?

Here the paragraph is still in the third person, but the point of view (also called the *means of perception*) has shifted to a different character. The entire story could be presented consistently in this manner or, especially if this were a longer work, the author might alternate between the two men.

In addition, third-person writing almost always contains at least some information which comes from the author directly.

(D)

They had known each other too long to see it, but over the years they had come to resemble each other in speech and dress. They even thought alike.

The person and the means of perception are interlocked. Together, they form the way in which a particular work of fiction is presented. I will develop this further in Chapter 7. For now, keep this in mind: It is important to notice right from the start how a story or novel is being presented. It will affect everything that follows.

What's happening?

On the simplest level, this is plot. Since most short stories and contemporary novels begin abruptly without leisurely introductions, you may have to make a special effort to find out exactly what has happened up to that point.

Occasionally a work of fiction will begin with what in television is called a *hook*. This is an extreme version of the abrupt opening—a scene which is dramatic in order to create interest and fails to give any background. In these cases, don't bother to keep reading over that first page. You can assume that the background to the situation will be filled in later. But stay alert to whatever hints may be given. Make sure you are making use of all the information the author has provided.

Even in more conventional openings, remember that a good deal of the background may be given indirectly through what characters say. For this reason you should pay particular attention to the dialogue at the opening of any story or novel.

PRACTICE

The way you start a new story or novel may determine the way you will read the entire work. If you begin in a casual manner, you will probably continue being a passive reader through to the end. If you ask yourself the right questions at the outset, however, you will begin the new work in an active way.

These five questions are not intended as merely a checklist to be memorized. Think of them as a set of concerns which will help you move into any new work of fiction rapidly and effectively. With a little practice, they will become automatic. Here is one way to speed the process:

Read the opening page of two different stories included in this volume. Try to answer the five questions on the basis of that much reading: Who's involved? Where are we? When is this? How is this being told? What's happening? Naturally, you will have more information in some areas than in others.

Next, take some brief but legible notes on these initial impressions so that you will have a record. Later, when you have had a chance to read both stories in their entirety, review your notes. Try to determine how these initial factors influenced the work as a whole.

If you repeat this same sequence with the other two stories included here or with any two selections in an anthology, the five critical questions will no longer seem like a formal list; they will become a way of staying alert, an attitude which you can adopt not only when beginning new stories but when reading novels as well.

Keep in mind that active reading is analytical reading, and the analysis should begin at once. Don't worry about spoiling the pleasure with too much thought. The closer you examine a work of literature, the more you will find to enjoy.

chapter 2

THE SOJOURNER

a story by Carson McCullers

The twilight border between sleep and waking was a Roman one this morning: splashing fountains and arched, narrow streets, the golden lavish city of blossoms and age-soft stone. Sometimes in this semi-consciousness he sojourned again in Paris, or war German rubble, or Swiss skiing and a snow hotel. Sometimes, also, in a fallow Georgia field at hunting dawn. Rome it was this morning in the yearless region of dreams.

John Ferris awoke in a room in a New York hotel. He had the feeling that something unpleasant was awaiting him—what it was, he did not know. The feeling, submerged by matinal necessities, lingered even after he had dressed and gone downstairs. It was a cloudless autumn day and the pale sunlight sliced between the pastel skyscrapers. Ferris went into the next-door drugstore and sat at the end booth next to the window glass that overlooked the sidewalk. He ordered an American breakfast with scrambled eggs and sausage.

Ferris had come from Paris to his father's funeral which had taken place the week before in his home town in Georgia. The shock of death had made him aware of youth already passed. His hair was receding and the veins in his now naked temples were pulsing and prominent and his body was spare except for an incipient belly bulge. Ferris had loved his father and the bond between them had once been extraordinarily close—but the years had somehow unraveled this filial devotion; the death, expected for a long time, had left him with an unforeseen dismay. He had stayed as long as possible to be near his mother and brothers at home. His plane for Paris was to leave the next morning.

Ferris pulled out his address book to verify a number. He turned the pages with growing attentiveness. Names and addresses from New York, the capitals of Europe, a few faint ones from his home state in the South. Faded, printed names, sprawled drunken ones. Betty Wills: a random love, married now. Charlie Williams: wounded in the Hürtgen Forest, unheard of since. Grand old Williams—did he live or die? Don Walker: a B.T.O. in television, getting rich. Henry Green: hit the skids after the war, in a sanitarium now, they say. Cozie Hall: he had heard that she was dead. Heedless, laughing Cozie—it was strange to think that she too, silly girl, could die. As Ferris closed the address book, he suffered a sense of hazard, transience, almost of fear.

It was then that his body jerked suddenly. He was staring out of the window when there, on the sidewalk, passing by, was his ex-wife. Elizabeth passed quite close to him, walking slowly. He could not understand the wild quiver of his heart, nor the following sense of recklessness and grace that lingered after she was gone.

Quickly Ferris paid his check and rushed out to the sidewalk. Elizabeth stood on the corner waiting to cross Fifth Avenue. He hurried toward her meaning to speak, but the lights changed and she crossed the street before he reached her. Ferris followed. On the other side he could easily have overtaken her, but he found himself lagging unaccountably. Her fair brown hair was plainly rolled, and as he watched her Ferris recalled that once his father had remarked that Elizabeth had a 'beautiful carriage.' She turned at the next corner and Ferris followed, although by now his intention to overtake her had disappeared. Ferris questioned the bodily disturbance that the sight of Elizabeth aroused in him, the dampness of his hands, the hard heartstrokes.

It was eight years since Ferris had last seen his ex-wife. He knew that long ago she had married again. And there were children. During recent years he had seldom thought of her. But at first, after the divorce, the loss had almost destroyed him. Then after the anodyne of time, he had loved again, and then again. Jeannine, she was now. Certainly his love for his ex-wife was long since past. So why the unhinged body, the shaken mind? He knew only that his clouded heart was oddly dissonant with the sunny, candid autumn day. Ferris wheeled suddenly and, walking with long strides, almost running, hurried back to the hotel.

Ferris poured himself a drink, although it was not yet eleven o'clock. He sprawled out in an armchair like a man exhausted, nursing his glass of bourbon and water. He had a full day ahead of him as he was leaving by plane the next morning for Paris. He checked over his obligations: take luggage to Air France, lunch with his boss, buy shoes and an overcoat. And something—wasn't there something else? Ferris finished his drink and opened the telephone directory.

His decision to call his ex-wife was impulsive. The number was under Bailey, the husband's name, and he called before he had much time for self-debate. He and Elizabeth had exchanged cards at Christmastime, and Ferris had sent a carving set when he received the announcement of her wedding. There was no reason *not* to call. But as he waited, listening to the ring at the other end, misgiving fretted him.

Elizabeth answered; her familiar voice was a fresh shock to him. Twice he had to repeat his name, but when he was identified, she sounded glad. He explained he was only in town for that day. They had a theater engagement, she said—but she wondered if he would come by for an early dinner. Ferris said he would be delighted.

As he went from one engagement to another, he was still bothered at odd moments by the feeling that something necessary was forgotten. Ferris bathed and changed in the late afternoon, often thinking about Jeannine; he would be with her the following night. 'Jeannine,' he would say, 'I happened to run into my ex-wife when I was in New York. Had dinner with her. And her husband, of course. It was strange seeing her after all these years.'

Elizabeth lived in the East Fifties, and as Ferris taxied uptown he glimpsed at intersections the lingering sunset, but by the time he reached his destination it was already autumn dark. The place was a building with a marquee and a doorman, and the apartment was on the seventh floor.

'Come in, Mr. Ferris.'

Braced for Elizabeth or even the unimagined husband, Ferris was astonished by the freckled red-haired child; he had known of the children, but his mind had failed somehow to acknowledge them. Surprise made him step back awkwardly.

'This is our apartment,' the child said politely. 'Aren't you Mr. Ferris? I'm Billy. Come in.'

In the living room beyond the hall, the husband provided another surprise; he too had not been acknowledged emotionally. Bailey was a lumbering red-haired man with a deliberate manner. He rose and extended a welcoming hand.

'I'm Bill Bailey. Glad to see you. Elizabeth will be in, in a minute. She's finishing dressing.'

The last words struck a gliding series of vibrations, memories of the other years. Fair Elizabeth, rosy and naked before her bath. Half-dressed before the mirror of her dressing table, brushing her fine, chestnut hair. Sweet, casual intimacy, the soft-fleshed loveliness indisputably possessed. Ferris shrank from the unbidden memories and compelled himself to meet Bill Bailey's gaze.

'Billy, will you please bring that tray of drinks from the kitchen table?'

The child obeyed promptly, and when he was gone Ferris remarked conversationally, 'Fine boy you have there.'

'We think so.'

Flat silence until the child returned with a tray of glasses and a cocktail shaker of Martinis. With the priming drinks they pumped up conversation: Russia, they spoke of, and the New York rainmaking, and the apartment situation in Manhattan and Paris.

'Mr. Ferris is flying all the way across the ocean tomorrow,' Bailey said to the little boy who was perched on the arm of his chair, quiet and well behaved. 'I bet you would like to be a stowaway in his suitcase.'

Billy pushed back his limp bangs. 'I want to fly in an airplane and be a newspaperman like Mr. Ferris.' He added with sudden assurance, 'That's what I would like to do when I am big.'

Bailey said, 'I thought you wanted to be a doctor.'

'I do!' said Billy. 'I would like to be both. I want to be a atombomb scientist too.'

Elizabeth came in carrying in her arms a baby girl.

'Oh, John!' she said. She settled the baby in the father's lap. 'It's grand to see you. I'm awfully glad you could come.'

The little girl sat demurely on Bailey's knees. She wore a pale pink crepe de Chine frock, smocked around the yoke with rose, and a matching silk hair ribbon tying back her pale soft curls. Her skin was summer tanned and her brown eyes flecked with gold and laughing. When she reached up and fingered her father's horn-rimmed glasses, he took them off and let her look through them a moment. 'How's my old Candy?'

Elizabeth was very beautiful, more beautiful perhaps than he had ever realized. Her straight clean hair was shining. Her face was softer, glowing and serene. It was a madonna loveliness, dependent on the family ambiance.

'You've hardly changed at all,' Elizabeth said, 'but it has been a long time.'

'Eight years.' His hand touched his thinning hair self-consciously while further amenities were exchanged.

Ferris felt himself suddenly a spectator—an interloper among these Baileys. Why had he come? He suffered. His own life seemed so solitary, a fragile column supporting nothing amidst the wreckage of the years. He felt he could not bear much longer to stay in the family room.

He glanced at his watch. 'You're going to the theater?'

'It's a shame,' Elizabeth said, 'but we've had this engagement for more than a month. But surely, John, you'll be staying home one of these days before long. You're not going to be an expatriate, are you?'

'Expatriate,' Ferris repeated. 'I don't much like the word.'

'What's a better word?' she asked.

He thought for a moment. 'Sojourner might do.'

Ferris glanced again at his watch, and again Elizabeth apologized. 'If only we had known ahead of time—'

'I just had this day in town. I came home unexpectedly. You see, Papa died last week.'

'Papa Ferris is dead?'

'Yes, at Johns-Hopkins. He had been sick there nearly a year. The funeral was down home in Georgia.'

'Oh, I'm so sorry, John. Papa Ferris was always one of my favorite people.'

The little boy moved from behind the chair so that he could look into his mother's face. He asked, 'Who is dead?'

Ferris was oblivious to apprehension; he was thinking of his father's death. He saw again the outstretched body on the quilted silk within the coffin. The corpse flesh was bizarrely rouged and the familiar hands lay massive and joined above a spread of funeral roses. The memory closed and Ferris awakened to Elizabeth's calm voice.

'Mr. Ferris's father, Billy. A really grand person. Somebody you didn't know.'

'But why did you call him *Papa* Ferris?'

Bailey and Elizabeth exchanged a trapped look. It was Bailey who answered the questioning child. 'A long time ago,' he said, 'your mother and Mr. Ferris were once married. Before you were born—a long time ago.'

'Mr. Ferris?'

The little boy stared at Ferris, amazed and unbelieving. And Ferris's eyes, as he returned the gaze, were somehow unbelieving too. Was it indeed true that at one time he had called this stranger, Elizabeth, Little Butterduck during nights of love, that they had lived together, shared perhaps a thousand days and nights and—finally—endured in the misery of sudden solitude the fiber by fiber (jealousy, alcohol and money quarrels) destruction of the fabric of married love.

Bailey said to the children, 'It's somebody's suppertime. Come on now.'

'But Daddy! Mama and Mr. Ferris—I—'

Billy's everlasting eyes—perplexed and with a glimmer of hostility—reminded Ferris of the gaze of another child. It was the young son of Jeannine—a boy of seven with a shadowed little face and knobby knees whom Ferris avoided and usually forgot.

'Quick march!' Bailey gently turned Billy toward the door. 'Say good night now, son.'

'Good night, Mr. Ferris.' He added resentfully, 'I thought I was staying up for the cake.'

'You can come in afterward for the cake,' Elizabeth said. 'Run along now with Daddy for your supper.'

Ferris and Elizabeth were alone. The weight of the situation descended on those first moments of silence. Ferris asked permission to pour himself another drink and Elizabeth set the cocktail shaker on the table at his side. He looked at the grand piano and noticed the music on the rack.

'Do you still play as beautifully as you used to?'

'I still enjoy it.'

'Please play, Elizabeth.'

Elizabeth arose immediately. Her readiness to perform when asked had always been one of her amiabilities; she never hung back, apologized. Now as she approached the piano there was the added readiness of relief.

She began with a Bach prelude and fugue. The prelude was as gaily iridescent as a prism in a morning room. The first voice of the fugue, an announcement pure and solitary, was repeated intermingling with a second voice, and again repeated within an elaborated frame, the multiple music, horizontal and serene, flowed with unhurried majesty. The principal melody was woven with two other voices, embellished with countless ingenuities—now dominant, again submerged, it had the sublimity of a single thing that does not fear surrender to the whole. Toward the end, the density of the material gathered for the last enriched insistence on the dominant first motif and with a chorded final statement the fugue ended. Ferris rested his head on the chair back and closed his eyes. In the following silence a clear, high voice came from the room down the hall.

'Daddy, how *could* Mama and Mr. Ferris—' A door was closed.

The piano began again—what was this music? Unplaced, familiar, the limpid melody had lain a long while dormant in his heart. Now it spoke to him of another time, another place—it was the music Elizabeth used to play. The delicate air summoned a wilderness of memory. Ferris was lost in the riot of past longings, conflicts, ambivalent desires. Strange that the music, catalyst for this tumultuous anarchy, was so serene and clear. The singing melody was broken off by the appearance of the maid.

'Miz Bailey, dinner is out on the table now.'

Even after Ferris was seated at the table between his host and hostess, the unfinished music still overcast his mood. He was a little drunk.

'*L'improvisation de la vie humaine,*'[1] he said. 'There's nothing that makes you so aware of the improvisation of human existence as a song unfinished. Or an old address book.'

'Address book?' repeated Bailey. Then he stopped, noncommittal and polite.

'You're still the same old boy, Johnny,' Elizabeth said with a trace of the old tenderness.

It was a Southern dinner that evening, and the dishes were his old favorites. They had fried chicken and corn pudding and rich, glazed candied sweet potatoes. During the meal Elizabeth kept alive a conversation when the silences were overlong. And it came about that Ferris was led to speak of Jeannine.

'I first knew Jeannine last autumn—about this time of the year—in Italy. She's a singer and she had an engagement in Rome. I expect we will be married soon.'

The words seemed so true, inevitable, that Ferris did not at first acknowledge to himself the lie. He and Jeannine had never in that year spoken of marriage. And indeed, she was still married—to a White Russian money-changer in Paris from whom she had been separated for five years. But it was too late to correct the lie. Already Elizabeth was saying: 'This really makes me glad to know. Congratulations, Johnny.'

He tried to make amends with truth. 'The Roman autumn is so beautiful. Balmy and blossoming.' He added, 'Jeannine has a little boy of six. A curious trilingual little fellow. We go to the Tuileries[2] sometimes.'

A lie again. He had taken the boy once to the gardens. The sallow foreign child in shorts that bared his spindly legs had sailed his boat in the concrete pond and ridden the pony. The child had wanted to go in to the puppet show. But there was not time, for Ferris had an engagement at the Scribe Hotel. He had promised

[1]The improvisation of human existence.

[2]A park in Paris.

they would go to the guignol[3] another afternoon. Only once had he taken Valentin to the Tuileries.

There was a stir. The maid brought in a white-frosted cake with pink candles. The children entered in their night clothes. Ferris still did not understand.

'Happy birthday, John,' Elizabeth said. 'Blow out the candles.'

Ferris recognized his birthday date. The candles blew out lingeringly and there was the smell of burning wax. Ferris was thirty-eight years old. The veins in his temples darkened and pulsed visibly.

'It's time you started for the theater.'

Ferris thanked Elizabeth for the birthday dinner and said the appropriate good-byes. The whole family saw him to the door.

A high, thin moon shone above the jagged, dark skyscrapers. The streets were windy, cold. Ferris hurried to Third Avenue and hailed a cab. He gazed at the nocturnal city with the deliberate attentiveness of departure and perhaps farewell. He was alone. He longed for flighttime and the coming journey.

The next day he looked down on the city from the air, burnished in sunlight, toylike, precise. Then America was left behind and there was only the Atlantic and the distant European shore. The ocean was milky pale and placid beneath the clouds. Ferris dozed most of the day. Toward dark he was thinking of Elizabeth and the visit of the previous evening. He thought of Elizabeth among her family with longing, gentle envy and inexplicable regret. He sought the melody, the unfinished air, that had so moved him. The cadence, some unrelated tones, were all that remained; the melody itself evaded him. He had found instead the first voice of the fugue that Elizabeth had played—it came to him, inverted mockingly and in a minor key. Suspended above the ocean the anxieties of transience and solitude no longer troubled him and he thought of his father's death with equanimity. During the dinner hour the plane reached the shore of France.

At midnight Ferris was in a taxi crossing Paris. It was a clouded night and mist wreathed the lights of the Place de la Concorde. The midnight bistros gleamed on the wet pavements. As always after a transocean flight the change of continents was too sudden. New York at morning, this midnight Paris. Ferris glimpsed the disorder of his life: the succession of cities, of transitory loves; and time, the sinister glissando of the years, time always.

'Vite! Vite!' he called in terror. 'Dépêchez-vous.'[4]

---

[3] A puppet show.
[4] "Quick! Quick! . . . . Hurry up."

Valentin opened the door to him. The little boy wore pajamas and an outgrown red robe. His grey eyes were shadowed and, as Ferris passed into the flat, they flickered momentarily.

'*J'attends Maman.*'[5]

Jeannine was singing in a night club. She would not be home before another hour. Valentin returned to a drawing, squatting with his crayons over the paper on the floor. Ferris looked down at the drawing—it was a banjo player with notes and wavy lines inside a comic-strip balloon.

'We will go again to the Tuileries.'

The child looked up and Ferris drew him closer to his knees. The melody, the unfinished music that Elizabeth had played, came to him suddenly. Unsought, the load of memory jettisoned—this time bringing only recognition and sudden joy.

'Monsieur Jean,' the child said, 'did you see him?'

Confused, Ferris thought only of another child—the freckled, family-loved boy. 'See who, Valentin?'

'Your dead papa in Georgia.' The child added, 'Was he okay?'

Ferris spoke with rapid urgency: 'We will go often to the Tuileries. Ride the pony and we will go into the guignol. We will see the puppet show and never be in a hurry any more.'

'Monsieur Jean,' Valentin said. 'The guignol is now closed.'

Again, the terror the acknowledgment of wasted years and death. Valentin, responsive and confident, still nestled in his arms. His cheek touched the soft cheek and felt the brush of the delicate eyelashes. With inner desperation he pressed the child close—as though an emotion as protean as his love could dominate the pulse of time.

[5]"I'm waiting for Mama."

chapter 3

THE CHARACTERS

CHARACTERS
AND CHARACTERIZATION
IN FICTION

Characters are the core of almost all sophisticated fiction. Even when we are uncertain about the theme of a new work, our attention is held if the characters are vivid. And long after we have finished a story or novel, we often recall certain characters even more clearly than the plot. In some cases, it is as if we had come to know a real person.

This is one of the significant differences between sophisticated (that is, literary) works and those which are simple. Adventure stories, gothic novels, and many television dramas depend on plot, not character. Plot is important in literary works as well, but in most cases it is the subtle development of character which holds our attention.

We use the word *character* in two somewhat different ways. The first refers simply to the fictionalized individuals who appear in stories, novels, or plays—"There are three characters in this story." The other includes aspects of personality and distinctive traits—"Her character is marked by courage and reserve." Normally the intended meaning is clear enough from the context, but the distinction is an important one.

It is natural enough to think about fictional characters as if they were people you have recently met. This is a good way to begin analyzing a story or novel as long as you don't get sidetracked on personal preferences. What a character is really like, whether he or she is essentially kind or thoughtless, mature or immature, honest or evasive—all these are important and interesting.

It is equally valuable to examine *characterization.* Strictly speaking, this term describes the portrayal or delineation of character. We might, for example, describe the *character* of John Ferris in Carson McCuller's story "The Sojourner" as outgoing, congenial, yet in some respects immature. His *characterization,* on the other hand, could be described as a contrast between an outward appearance of relaxed self-assurance shown mainly through action and dialogue and, on the other hand, an uneasiness about his rootless existence and advancing age revealed primarily through thoughts. The word *characterization* usually focuses on the ways in which character is revealed.

There is no limit to the variety of techniques associated with characterization, but they can be grouped under five headings or *narrative modes:* action, dialogue, thoughts, description, and exposition. When we read rapidly, we are hardly aware that these five narrative modes are being used in quick succession to reveal the complex nature of a character. But when we analyze a work in depth, it is helpful to isolate and identify them. This chapter deals with both characters and methods of characterization.

FLAT VERSUS ROUND CHARACTERS

These somewhat whimsical-sounding terms are very useful. They were introduced by E. M. Forster in *Aspects of the Novel.* They distinguish characters who are never developed in depth from those who are.

Almost every work of fiction has *flat* characters. We refer to them as "minor" characters, but often they serve an important function in the development of a story or novel.

This is certainly the case in "The Sojourner." Elizabeth's husband, Bill Bailey, and the two children are flat in the sense that they are not developed. We are not given any direct view of their thoughts and we have very little information about their attitudes. We know only that Bill appears amiable and the children well-behaved. They don't do anything to alter the course of events, and they don't reveal any change in outlook or attitude. They are essentially static. But in spite of this they are essential elements in the story because they illustrate the solid, secure family life which Elizabeth now has and which John Ferris does not. Bill Bailey and his two children are not there just for decoration; they provide the model which John may try to use—rather belatedly—in his relationship with Jeannine and her son in Paris.

One way to test the importance of flat characters is to imagine the story without them. The author could have had John Ferris and Elizabeth meet for dinner by themselves in some restaurant, eliminating the husband and children entirely. The final scenes could have been left exactly the same, preserving the original plot. But we would lose that picture of stable, harmonious family life which has such an effect on Ferris.

Flat characters, then, are like cardboard cutouts in that we don't see more than one side of them. They rarely change or develop in any significant way. But as we have seen they can have an important part to play in a story or novel. They may even be pivotal, causing some major turn of events. This is why the term *flat* is more accurate than *minor*.

Don't confuse flat characters with *stock characters*. A stock character is a *cliché*. Slick fiction and many television dramas and sitcoms are built on stock characters who behave in a predictable manner. They conform to a *stereotype*, a cartoon-like notion such as "the tough cop," the "wise-guy taxi driver," and the like. Flat characters in sophisticated fiction are more individualized, more credible, even though we see only one side of them.

A *round* character is by definition multidimensional—that is, we can see more than one side of his or her personality. The portrayal has to be more penetrating than "the tough cop with a heart of gold." That's merely a stock character made slightly more interesting. Round characters have the rich variety of qualities and attitudes which we see in those we know well. They can't be summed up in a single sentence any more than our close friends can.

In addition, a round character is usually *dynamic* rather than *static*. That is, he or she changes an attitude, grows, develops, or weakens under this or that circumstance. This kind of development is often central to the work.

Occasionally it is the reader's view of the character which changes or develops. The unfolding of the story or novel may reveal the *protagonist* or central character slowly and in layers, like peeling an onion. When this is handled with some subtlety and insight, it becomes another way of creating a round character.

John Ferris in "The Sojourner" is a good example of a round character. He is being pulled in two directions, and even at the end of the story he is a mix of the wanderer and one who longs for the stability and comfort of a permanent relationship. It is not a dramatic change of personality (few short stories attempt this); but when you compare the subtle shifts which are revealed in his attitude with the entirely static picture we have of Bill Bailey, you can appreciate the difference between characters who are round and those who are flat.

THE ILLUSION OF REALITY

When characters appear "real" and stay in the memory as if we had actually met them, the illusion is created by a combination of three factors: *consistency, complexity,* and *individuality.* All fully developed characters are made up of a combination of these three—though not in the same proportion. We come to understand a work far more fully when we analyze the degree to which each has been used.

Consistency

Consistency is what makes a character "hang together" in a logical way. It rarely is the whole personality—in fiction or in life. We may say of a friend, "She's easygoing and sociable," or of another, "He's a loner," but we don't mean that such brief appraisals describe the whole person. Such phrases merely serve as a kind of "handle" with which to identify the individual.

In simple fiction (adventure stories, for example, or costume gothic novels), characters are portrayed with a high degree of consistency. Good characters remain good; the evil stay evil (or reform and become totally good on the last page). And even though flat characters in literature are more realistic, they are also presented as highly consistent.

Although we associate consistency with flat characters, remember that it is a necessary element in those who are fully developed as well. Round characters may act in ways which are surprising, but their actions are rarely left unexplained. When a character makes some significant decision at the end of a story or novel or behaves in a way which is unexpected, you can almost always find details earlier in the work which provide a forewarning. Some degree of consistency is necessary just to maintain credibility.

Complexity

Complexity is what creates a round or fully developed character. We have to be able to see variations and even contradictions in behavior and attitude before we have the sense of knowing a character in depth.

Rather than being all good or all bad, fully developed characters are usually some of each. They are also likely to be a mix of maturity and immaturity, innocence and sophistication, self-centeredness and warmth. John Ferris in "The Sojourner," for example, is both an independent individual who has avoided responsibilities and one who is reaching out for some type of long-range relationship. Which is the "real" John Ferris? Both.

In addition to personal qualities, a character's attitude may be contradictory. Someone may be liberal in principle but biased about who lives next door. A husband may be kind and forgiving with his mother but thoughtless with his wife. A businessperson may be genuinely honest in personal relations yet dishonest at work—or the reverse.

Remember that in fiction as in life an individual can hold two opposing emotions at the same time. This is referred to as *ambivalence* and can be a quick flash of a feeling such as the combination of rage and love a parent might feel when the child who was thought to be lost was in fact only hiding. But more often it is sustained, as in the mix of love and resentment many people feel for a parent or other relative, the fear and fascination some mountain climbers feel toward the risks they must take, the feeling of respect and hatred many sports figures and politicians feel for their opponents.

Another form of complexity is what is sometimes referred to as *character change*. The term is somewhat misleading since it rarely takes the form of a basic shift in personality. Comedies occasionally have such fundamental transformations in the concluding scenes, but serious, sophisticated fiction tends to suggest changes in attitude which are more subtle and realistic.

This is certainly the case with John Ferris in "The Sojourner." The author does not have him do a complete about-face. It would be pleasant but hardly credible to have him suddenly decide to marry, settle down, and be a good parent to his stepson. Such an "easy" resolution is one of the characteristics of slick fiction, adventure stories, and television dramas in which the gang leader becomes a drug counselor and the wife beater becomes a model husband.

Carson McCullers, on the other hand, is concerned with creating a character who is closer to the subtleties and uncertainties of our own lives. Ferris is clearly affected by his experiences at the end of the story, but whether he will transform his life or not remains open to question.

The process of change in this story is almost more important than the change itself. It has already begun as the story opens. Although we have no way of knowing its significance at first, the funeral of his father has been a sharp reminder to Ferris that he is growing older and that his life, too, is limited. When he sees Elizabeth with her family, this uneasy sense of passing time grows. We know this not through direct analysis but from his statement that he is about to get married, a casual but significant lie. He is again dishonest when he describes taking Jeannine's boy to the park a number of times. These deceits suggest how Ferris' attitude is changing. They reveal a direction he would now like to take—if it is not too late.

At the end of the story we are reminded once again of the funeral which was first mentioned in the opening. The child, Valentin, innocently asks about Ferris' father and Ferris experiences, once again, "the terror the acknowledgment of wasted years and death." He embraces the child "as though an emotion as protean as his love could dominate the pulse of

time." The author is suggesting that Ferris' love is highly changeable (protean) and does not have the power to stop the advance of time. There is complexity in the way this character has altered his perceptions about the good life, but there is consistency too—perhaps too much to enable him to alter his life in any fundamental way.

Individuality

The third element in the illusion of reality is *individuality*. This is what makes the character memorable. We have all been to parties in which we have met a number of new people only one of whom we can remember by name the next day. Why that one? It may have been that he or she had a strong set of convictions, a good sense of humor, or leads an interesting life. In many cases, however, it is because either knowingly or unknowingly this individual revealed a good deal about his or her personal feelings.

John Ferris in "The Sojourner" may not be what one thinks of as a strong individual, but his character is revealed in such a way as to make him memorable. That opening paragraph which describes "the twilight border between sleep and waking" suggests a man who leads a rather exotic life— images of Rome, Paris, Germany, and Switzerland. This is the kind of individuality which is often used to arouse our interest in the protagonists of slick fiction. But it is not long before we learn more penetrating details about John Ferris: that he is unsure about his life and that he is directionless and essentially rootless. In addition, he is increasingly aware that his life is passing by and that he, like his father before him, will face death.

If you met such a character at a party you might be initially intrigued by the sophisticated life he leads. He has been around. But if you learned as much about his inner makeup as you do from the story, you would most certainly never forget him. In life, we rarely find out so much about a person in so short a period of time, but sophisticated fiction is designed to reveal a great deal extremely rapidly. It is the degree of our insight which makes a character truly memorable.

Individuality in sophisticated fiction, then, is not achieved merely by having a character lead a life which is exciting or exotic. In the stories you will be reading in this volume, one protagonist is an unemployed black man, another is an elderly owner of a fish-packing plant, and a third is an adolescent working in a supermarket. None of them leads what you might think of as an exciting life. But in each case you are given vivid insights into a life which is clearly unique. As a result, each character is highly individualized and is, for most readers, memorable.

You will get much more from any novel or story if you take the time to examine each rounded character while you are reading and again when you have finished. Start with a brief, general statement as if you were telling a friend what that person was like. Then identify the variations and

complications. Finally, consider the reasons this character will probably stay in your memory. In this way you will have examined the ways in which that character was consistent, complex, and memorable.

TECHNIQUES
OF CHARACTERIZATION

To this point we have been examining fictional characters as if they were people we have just met—which in one sense they are. But how did we learn so much about them so quickly? We now turn to the literary devices which are used in fiction to reveal character.

When you read passively, your mind naturally focuses on content, not technique. You are concentrating on *what* a character is like, not *how* that character is being revealed. Only when you read actively can you begin to take pleasure in the intricacies of characterization. The best approach is to look closely at the author's use of the five *narrative modes:* action, dialogue, thoughts, description, and exposition.

Action

Action is in some respects the least subtle of these narrative modes. Action is the dominant mode in adventure stories as well as in television dramas which so often follow the same patterns. Certain types of action are used repeatedly to communicate specific moods. When we see a character pound the wall, we don't have to be told that he or she is angry; when two characters embrace, we assume affection. The high-speed auto chase is a standard method of communicating tension. Stories and novels which are based on a succession of such highly dramatic but familiar scenes are described as "action-packed" and are often lacking in the development of character and theme.

But action can be used in a sophisticated way to reveal even the most complex fictional character. Look at how we come to understand the rootlessness of John Ferris in "The Sojourner." He has recently flown from Paris to attend a funeral in Georgia; at the opening of the story he is in New York City; and at the end of the story he flies back to Paris. All this restless motion gives us a better sense of what his life is like than if the author had merely told us, "He was always on the go." One way to appreciate what that type of action does to help us understand the character of Ferris is to imagine the story revised so that he had been quietly living in another part of the city all those years. The plot would remain essentially unchanged, but our understanding of the ways in which he is a "sojourner" would be severely limited. In fact, even the title might have to be changed.

Action can also take the form of small and apparently insignificant

details. When, for example, John Ferris is told by Elizabeth, "You've hardly changed at all," he responds with a simple gesture: "His hand touched his thinning hair self-consciously." It is one of several little reminders that this character is thinking about how time is passing him by. Later, when the surprise birthday cake is brought in (itself a significant bit of action dealing with the passage of time), we are told that "The veins in his temples darkened and pulsed visibly." The author doesn't have to tell us, "This was an emotional experience for him"; we recognize it just as we might in life—through a minor and involuntary bit of action.

Dialogue

Dialogue, the second narrative mode, almost always reveals more about the fictional speaker than does normal daily conversation. What characters say is usually designed to reflect aspects of personality (self-assurance, insecurity, egotism, lack of self-esteem, and the like). It can also be used to reveal a character's mood (confident, uncertain, and so forth).

When reading dialogue, keep track of who is listening. Characters, like people, often adapt their words to their hearers depending on their relationship and on what kind of an impression they hope to make.

When John Ferris lies, for example, saying that he and Jeannine plan to get married, he is describing himself to the Baileys as more settled than he really is. He is also revealing a desire to capture some of the domestic harmony and companionship he sees in Elizabeth's family. And when in that final scene he promises to take young Valentin to the park for pony rides and puppet shows, he reveals both his good intentions and his lack of foresight, for the puppet show ("the guignol") has been closed for the season.

Thoughts

Thoughts are in many respects similar to dialogue. They reveal aspects of character as well as immediate feelings. Occasionally they contradict what a character is saying and thus show a contrast between what he or she is willing to reveal and what is really going through the mind.

A character's thoughts are usually quoted directly as if they were lines of dialogue—though generally without quotation marks. For example:

> I'm nothing but a spectator, he thought. I'm just an interloper among these Baileys. Why did I come? They make me feel isolated. What have I got to show for all these years? I can't stick around here much longer.

Another approach is to describe thoughts indirectly, using the third person. Here is this same passage converted from direct to indirect thoughts. Can you tell which of these two versions is the one used by Carson McCullers in "The Sojourner?"

Ferris felt himself suddenly a spectator—an interloper among these Baileys. Why had he come? He suffered. His own life seemed so solitary, a fragile column supporting nothing amidst the wreckage of the years. He felt he could not bear much longer to stay in the family room.

Carson McCullers decided to use indirect thoughts, the second, perhaps because it gave her the chance to comment a bit on Ferris' reactions. It also allowed her to use phrasing which is slightly more complex than what might flash through his mind. It seems unlikely, for example, that he would actually think to himself, "My life is a fragile column supporting nothing amidst the wreckage of the years." This is more plausibly the phrasing of an author describing indirectly the feelings of a character. In this respect, thoughts which are reported indirectly begin to resemble exposition, a narrative mode which I will describe shortly.

Description

The fourth narrative mode is *description*. Sometimes characters themselves are described in ways which give us hints about their personalities or inner concerns. John Ferris' uneasiness about his advancing age, for example, is reflected in his "thinning hair"; Elizabeth's inner harmony is shown through her simple beauty ("Her face was softer, glowing and serene . . . . a madonna loveliness, dependent on the family ambiance"), and Bill Bailey's reliability is seen in his description as "a lumbering red-haired man with a deliberate manner." We know that in life it is often a mistake to judge a person by his or her appearance, and of course this can be true in fiction too. But even if you as reader are being led astray, remember that this too is part of the author's intent.

Descriptive passages which reveal character do not have to be limited to personal appearances. Occasionally they focus on something closely associated with an individual. There is an extraordinary example of this in "The Sojourner." The author describes the Bach prelude and fugue which Elizabeth plays on the piano, and that description becomes an intricate picture of Elizabeth and her marriage. It begins with a "pure and solitary" voice which is then heard "intermingling with a second voice," and finally becomes "woven with two other voices, embellished with countless ingenuities." The passage is a highly poetic metaphor for Elizabeth's life as a single person who is soon joined by "a second voice," her new husband, and then two children in a harmonious family unit. If you skipped over that description in your first reading, you may wish to review it now (see p. 14).

Exposition

Exposition is the fifth narrative mode used to reveal fictional characters. It is also called "direct analysis." In earlier centuries such passages were often used extensively and were unmistakably from the author's point of view. Here is a sample from W. M. Thackeray's *Vanity Fair:*

> But wherever she went she touched and charmed every one of the male sex. . . . I think it was her weakness which was her principal charm.

The "I" here is the author and the passage is clearly an opinion given by him. It provides not only an aspect of character but an opinion as well. It is similar to phrasing we might use when speaking aloud.

In the twentieth century, however, authors tend to avoid direct analysis of their characters. Although there are interesting exceptions (Donald Barthelme and Margaret Drabble are good examples), most authors refrain from using their own "voices" directly in their fiction. When they do provide information about their characters directly, it is apt to be factual and often incidental information. This means that they, like dramatists, have come to rely more heavily on action and dialogue to reveal the true nature of their characters. As readers, then, we should be particularly concerned with what a character does and says—just as we are in life.

TAKING NOTES

If you are studying a work of fiction carefully, you will want to take notes. As I have mentioned before, merely writing them helps to organize and record your impressions in your memory even if you never refer to them. Also, when you do take notes, the characters will be just as important as the plot and the theme.

To save time, keep your notes brief. A thumbnail sketch (a few precise phrases) on each major character is usually enough. Don't forget to include how you discovered important aspects of that character—the characterization. We all have different ways of taking notes, but here is a sample of what one might record for "The Sojourner":

JOHN FERRIS

lives abroad
never settled down (a foreign correspondent?)
divorced 8 years
worried about passing years (thinning hair; thoughts of death and marriage)
may not be able to settle down
(effort to be close to Valentin not very successful)

ELIZABETH BAILEY

ex-wife of Ferris
married and content

still fond of Ferris (made birthday cake)
seems to have a good life (note description of the music she plays)

You may prefer to use more formal headings with numbered sub-headings, but whatever your approach, consider these general guidelines: Notes on the characters should be clear (not scribbled in the margins), precise (not vague generalities), and detailed enough to sharpen your memory at a later date. The style you adopt is up to you, but remember that what you write should be meaningful and helpful weeks later.

TOPICS FOR ANALYSIS

The following five essay questions are intended primarily to suggest topics for short papers. Advice on how to write good papers appears in Chapter 16. These questions can also be used as the basis of a discussion or merely to sharpen your own thinking about what you have read.

1.   Imagine "The Sojourner" written from the point of view of Bill Bailey, giving his thoughts and feelings rather than those of Ferris. He would then become a round character and John Ferris flat. What new insights might we make about Bailey (and perhaps his wife)? What aspects of Ferris would we lose? (You may find that this changes the very theme of the story!)

2.   Select another story or a scene from a novel which contains both a round and a flat character. Analyze what changes would occur if the work developed the minor character so that we saw the scene from that person's point of view and learned about his or her inner feelings.

3.   Describe a character in a story or novel not discussed here. Write your description without direct reference to the work of fiction, pretending that this is a person you have recently come to know. Now write a precise analysis of the details in the story or novel which gave you that impression. Be very specific and identify in each case whether the evidence from the work of fiction is a detail of action, dialogue, thoughts, description, or exposition. Which of these narrative modes was the most helpful in giving you a picture of that character?

4.   Describe someone's room with such detail that your reader will know exactly what the owner is like. (If you begin with an actual room, remember that you are writing fiction and so can eliminate some aspects and invent others.)

5.   If the preceding topic has been selected by several students, here is a second stage: Exchange papers and write a monologue based on the character you feel was being described in the theme you received. Your best approach here would be to write a short sketch describing the fictional owner of that room before you begin your monologue. Feel free to exaggerate a bit. Enjoy yourself.

One final note on the subject of fictional characters: Whenever you read a story or novel, take a few moments to describe the major characters to yourself even if you are not planning to write a paper on that work. The simple act of working out a brief analysis will sharpen your perception. Then take a close look at the methods the author has used to develop that portrait. There is a natural tendency to recall a work of fiction in terms of plot, but it is the characters who give it depth.

chapter 4

ON THE ROAD

a story by Langston Hughes

He was not interested in the snow. When he got off the freight, one early evening during the depression, Sargeant never even noticed the snow. But he must have felt it seeping down his neck, cold, wet, sopping in his shoes. But if you had asked him, he wouldn't have known it was snowing. Sargeant didn't see the snow, not even under the bright lights of the main street, falling white and flaky against the night. He was too hungry, too sleepy, too tired.

The Reverend Mr. Dorset, however, saw the snow when he switched on his porch light, opened the front door of his parsonage, and found standing there before him a big black man with snow on his face, a human piece of night with snow on his face—obviously unemployed.

Said the Reverend Mr. Dorset before Sargeant even realized he'd opened his mouth: "I'm sorry. No! Go right on down this street four blocks and turn to your left, walk up seven, and you'll see the Relief Shelter. I'm sorry. No!" He shut the door.

Sargeant wanted to tell the holy man that he had already been to the Relief Shelter, been to hundreds of relief shelters during the depression years; the beds were always gone, and supper was over; the place was full, and they drew the color line anyhow. But the minister said, "No," and shut the door. Evidently he didn't want to hear about it. And he *had* a door to shut.

The big black man turned away. And even yet he didn't see the snow, walking right into it. Maybe he sensed it, cold, wet, sticking to his jaws, wet on his black hands, sopping in his shoes. He stopped and stood on the sidewalk hunched over—hungry, sleepy, cold—looking up and down. Then he looked right where he was—in front of a church. Of course! A church! Sure, right next to a parsonage, certainly a church.

It had *two* doors.

Broad white steps in the night all snowy white. Two high arched doors with slender stone pillars on either side. And way up, a round lacy window with a stone crucifix in the middle and Christ on the crucifix in stone. All this was pale in the street lights, solid and stony pale in the snow.

Sargeant blinked. When he looked up, the snow fell into his eyes. For the first time that night he *saw* the snow. He shook his head. He shook the snow from his coat sleeves, felt hungry, felt lost, felt not lost, felt cold. He walked up the steps of the church. He knocked at the door. No answer. He tried the handle. Locked. He put his shoulder against the door, and his long black body slanted like a ramrod. He pushed. With loud rhythmic grunts, like the grunts in a chain-gang song, he pushed against the door.

"I'm tired . . . Huh! . . . Hongry. . . Uh! . . . I'm sleepy. . . Huh! I'm cold . . . I got to sleep somewheres," Sargeant said. "This here is a church, ain't it? Well, uh!"

He pushed against the door.

Suddenly, with an undue cracking and screaking, the door began to give way to the tall black Negro who pushed ferociously against it.

By now two or three white people had stopped in the street, and Sargeant was vaguely aware of them yelling at him concerning the door. Three or four more came running, yelling at him.

"Hey!" they said. "Hey!"

"Uh-huh," answered the big tall Negro, "I know it's a white folks' church, but I got to sleep somewhere." He gave another lunge at the door. "Huh!"

And the door broke open.

But just when the door gave way, two white cops arrived in a car, ran up the steps with their clubs, and grabbed Sargeant. But Sargeant for once had no intention of being pulled or pushed away from the door.

Sargeant grabbed, but not for anything so weak as a broken door. He grabbed for one of the tall stone pillars beside the door, grabbed at it and caught it. And held it. The cops pulled and Sargeant pulled. Most of the people in the street got behind the cops and helped them pull.

"A big black unemployed Negro holding onto our church!" thought the people. "The idea!"

The cops began to beat Sargeant over the head, and nobody protested. But he held on.

And then the church fell down.

Gradually, the big stone front of the church fell down, the walls and the rafters, the crucifix and the Christ. Then the whole thing fell down, covering the cops and the people with bricks and stones and debris. The whole church fell down in the snow.

Sargeant got out from under the church and went walking on up the street with the stone pillar on his shoulder. He was under the impression that he had buried the parsonage and the Reverend Mr. Dorset who said, "No!" So he laughed and threw the pillar six blocks up the street and went on.

Sargeant thought he was alone, but listening to the *crunch, crunch, crunch* on the snow of his own footsteps, he heard other footsteps, too, doubling his own. He looked around, and there was Christ walking along beside him, the same Christ that had been on the cross on the church—still stone with a rough stone surface, walking along beside him just like he was broken off the cross when the church fell down.

"Well, I'll be dogged," said Sargeant. "This here's the first time I ever seed you off the cross."

"Yes," said Christ, crunching his feet in the snow. "You had to pull the church down to get me off the cross."

"You glad?" said Sargeant.

"I sure am," said Christ.

They both laughed.

"I'm a hell of a fellow, ain't I?" said Sargeant. "Done pulled the church down!"

"You did a good job," said Christ. "They have kept me nailed on a cross for nearly two thousand years."

"Whee-ee-e!" said Sargeant. "I know you are glad to get off."

"I sure am," said Christ.

They walked on in the snow. Sargeant looked at the man of stone.

"And you have been up there two thousand years?"

"I sure have," Christ said.

"Well, if I had a little cash," said Sargeant, "I'd show you around a bit."

"I been around," said Christ.

"Yeah, but that was a long time ago."

"All the same," said Christ, "I've been around."

They walked on in the snow until they came to the railroad yards. Sargeant was tired, sweating and tired.

"Where you goin?" Sargeant said, stopping by the tracks. He looked at Christ. Sargeant said, "I'm just a bum on the road. How about you? Where you goin'?"

"God knows," Christ said, "but I'm leavin' here."

They saw the red and green lights of the railroad yard half veiled by the snow that fell out of the night. Away down the track they saw a fire in a hobo jungle.

"I can go there and sleep," Sargeant said.

"You can?"

"Sure," said Sargeant. "That place ain't got no doors."

Outside the town, along the tracks, there were barren trees and bushes below the embankment, snow-gray in the dark. And down among the trees and bushes there were makeshift houses made out of boxes and tin and old pieces of wood and canvas. You couldn't see them in the dark, but you knew they were there if you'd ever been on the road, if you had ever lived with the homeless and hungry in a depression.

"I'm side-tracking," Sargeant said. "I'm tired."

"I'm gonna make it on to Kansas City," said Christ.

"O.K.," Sargeant said. "So long!"

He went down into the hobo jungle and found himself a place to sleep. He never did see Christ no more. About 6:00 A.M. a freight came by. Sargeant scrambled out of the jungle with a dozen or so more hobos and ran along the track, grabbing at the freight. It was dawn, cold and gray.

"Wonder where Christ is by now?" Sargeant thought. "He musta gone on way on down the road. He didn't sleep in this jungle."

Sargeant grabbed the train and started to pull himself up into a moving coal car, over the edge of a wheeling coal car. But strangely enough, the car was full of cops. The nearest cop rapped Sargeant soundly across the knuckles with his night stick. Wham! Rapped his big black hands for clinging to the top of the car. Wham! But Sargeant did not turn loose. He clung on and tried to pull himself into the car. He hollered at the top of his voice, "Damn it, lemme in this car!"

"Shut up," barked the cop. "You crazy coon!" He rapped Sargeant across the knuckles and punched him in the stomach. "You ain't out in no jungle now. This ain't no train. You in jail."

Wham! across his bare black fingers clinging to the bars of his cell. Wham! between the steel bars low down against his shins.

Suddenly Sargeant realized that he really was in jail. He wasn't on no train. The blood of the night before had dried on his face, his head hurt terribly, and a cop outside in the corridor was hitting him across the knuckles for holding onto the door, yelling and shaking the cell door.

"They musta took me to jail for breaking down the door last night," Sargeant thought, "that church door."

Sargeant went over and sat on a wooden bench against the cold stone wall. He was emptier than ever. His clothes were wet, clammy cold wet, and shoes sloppy with snow water. It was just about dawn. There he was, locked up behind a cell door, nursing his bruised fingers.

The bruised fingers were his, but not the *door.*

Not the *club,* but the fingers.

"You wait," mumbled Sargeant, black against the jail wall. "I'm gonna break down this door, too."

"Shut up—or I'll paste you one," said the cop.

"I'm gonna break down this door," yelled Sargeant as he stood up in his cell.

Then he must have been talking to himself because he said, "I wonder where Christ's gone? I wonder if he's gone to Kansas City?"

chapter 5

THE SETTING

*a sense of place: scope of the
    physical setting
temporal setting: time of day,
    season, historical period
social setting
examining the setting
topics for analysis*

Where are we? This is a natural question to ask as we begin a new work of fiction. We want to know where we are physically—in a city or the country, here or abroad, and the like. We also want to know about time—not just time of day, but the season and the historical period as well. Finally, we need to identify the social milieu.

Setting, then, has three related ways of orienting us as we read: *where* the story takes place—the physical setting; *when*—the temporal setting; and *with whom*—the social setting. Without these landmarks, a work of fiction would seem abstract and detached from common experience.

Most stories and novels establish the setting on the very first page. Sometimes this is done directly through description, but often it is handled so subtly that we are hardly aware of how we have been informed. If you are reading carefully, take a close look both at how the setting has been identified and, even more important, at how it is then used in the body of a work. Often the method used will have a direct bearing on the plot, the tone, and, most significant of all, the theme.

A SENSE OF PLACE

The degree to which the physical setting is used as a fictional device varies enormously. There are stories and novels in which the surroundings seem almost incidental. But at the other extreme there are works in which some aspect of setting—like a house, a ship, a storm, or a mountain—will be given all the significance of a fictional character. This is not a question of good technique or bad; it is merely a matter of artistic choice.

Scope of the physical setting

In addition to the degree to which setting has been emphasized in a particular work, there is the *scope*. Scope is the breadth of the setting—whether it portrays an entire nation, a region, a town, or is limited to a single room. At one end of the spectrum the author uses what might be thought of as a wide-angle lens. At the other extreme, the work reveals only a small area—though perhaps in great detail. These differing approaches are worth considering and applying to what you read.

The wide-angle approach lends itself to the novel form better than to stories. In many cases, novels using this approach are necessarily long. The author may attempt to depict national character as well as historical events during a particular period. Tolstoi's *War and Peace,* for example, is often called an "epic" work because of its panoramic scope. German history and culture are the subjects of a multigenerational novel by Thomas Mann entitled *Buddenbrooks.* Germany in the 1930s and 1940s is treated by Günter Grass in *The Tin Drum.* The South American scene over the course of a century is revealed in a fanciful yet ultimately serious work, *One Hundred Years of Solitude,* by Gabriel Garcia Marquez. The most ambitious attempt to depict the United States is a trilogy by John Dos Passos with the appropriate collective title of *U.S.A.*

These broad-scope novels share three characteristics: a large cast of characters, relatively complex, *multitrack* plots (discussed in Chapter 11), and a blending of actual history with fictitious events. This type of fiction has resulted in some of the most important novels ever written, but it is also imitated by commercial authors who are more concerned with simple entertainment and wide sales than with enrichment.

A majority of novels use a somewhat narrower scope. Their settings are limited to particular regions. The works of William Faulkner, for example, concentrate on the South. Willa Cather provides a penetrating view of the Southwest in *Death Comes for the Archbishop.* Joan Didion's satiric portrayal of West Coast life in *The White Album* is only one of many from that area. New England has been examined by a multitude of authors from Nathaniel Hawthorne and Herman Melville to such contemporary novelists as the satiric John P. Marquand and the chronicler of underworld life in Boston, George Higgins. Such writers help to define the particular characteristics of a region.

When a specific city is used for a setting, the scope is still more restricted. But the complexity of the urban scene is such that this is no limitation. If the city is a major one—particularly New York or Chicago—it is often named. Even readers who have not been there are apt to be familiar with their major landmarks. Smaller cities and towns are usually given fictitious names. In either case, the view of that setting is still fiction—that is, what we are shown has been filtered through the imagination of the author. It may not be accurate the way a historical account would be, but it draws on the real area to create its own vivid world.

The narrowest scope is seen in those works which are limited to a confined area. A ship, for example, has frequently been used. If you are interested in what can be done with such a restricted setting, read Joseph Conrad's *Youth* or Katherine Ann Porter's *A Ship of Fools.*

Short stories tend to have settings which are narrow in scope. There just isn't time to create a panoramic view. Yet these settings are often important. This is certainly the case in Carson McCullers' story, "The Sojourner." McCullers not only uses specific place names throughout the work, she also depends on them to develop a significant part of the theme. As John Ferris wakes, he sees images of Rome and we are told that often he dreams of Paris, Germany, Switzerland, and Georgia. In the next paragraph we learn that he is in a New York hotel. He has just been to Georgia and is about to fly back to Paris. As I pointed out in Chapter 3, such a variety of localities, all named specifically, gives us a sense of restless motion which helps us to understand Ferris' life and character. His rootlessness is contrasted with the stability and tranquility of Elizabeth and her family. The story doesn't make use of setting to reveal aspects of a particular region as, for example, many of Faulkner's do. But setting becomes a vehicle for developing character.

Some stories limit the setting to a particular house or even to a specific room. They are like stage plays which are limited to a single set. What is lost in breadth is often gained in minute details.

This approach is vividly illustrated in the next story you will read, "A & P" by John Updike. As the title suggests, almost the entire story takes place in a supermarket. Although there is a single reference indicating that the store is situated "north of Boston," little is made of this. The events could have occurred in any state from Hawaii to New Jersey. When you read this work, however, notice the astonishing number of visual details. Consider the ways in which this setting—the interior of a supermarket—becomes an important part of the theme itself. I will return to this point in Chapter 15, "Thematic Concerns."

Setting does not necessarily have to be realistic to be convincing. Some fiction places us in a dream world which, like real dreams, becomes intensely vivid. Here too the scope can be panoramic or narrow. Tolkien's trilogy, *The Lord of the Rings,* for example, creates a complex world with its own creatures and unique landscapes. At the other end of the scale are some of the fantasy stories of Franz Kafka which concentrate on a single room. We come to believe in such works not because the setting is similar to what we know but because it is internally consistent. We are transported to an environment which "makes sense" to our imaginations.

TEMPORAL SETTING

Although we tend to associate the term *setting* with a geographic area or place, it can also refer to time. This includes time of day, the season, and, on the broadest level, the historical period.

Time of day and season

Mornings bring to mind new plans and expectations—whether good or bad. Perhaps for this reason, opening scenes of stories are often set at that time of day. Nights can have quite different associations.

Carson McCullers makes use of both in "The Sojourner." At the beginning of the story, John Ferris wakes with a vague sense of foreboding. The final scene, set in Paris at midnight, explains that anxiety. The hour helps to dramatize his "inner desperation." True, the plot would not be damaged if he had arrived on a warm, sunny, spring morning; but what a difference it would have made to the tone of that ending!

Langston Hughes makes use of both the time of day and the season in "On the Road." The opening scene could have occurred on a sunny afternoon, but the darkness adds to the harsh tone. It could have taken place in summer, but then the author could not have used the symbolic detail of white snow falling on Sargeant's black face. Both the hour and the season have been selected not just to arouse your pity (that would create sentimentality), but to generate genuine indignation in the reader and to develop important symbolic details.

It is possible to write good fiction without identifying either the time of day or the season. But when such details do appear, look at them carefully. You may find that they are being used to develop the tone, a symbolic suggestion, or the theme of the work.

Historical period

The third form of temporal setting is historical period. Fiction can provide a marvelous view of life in the past. It is as close as we can get to a time machine. But there are certain obstacles which you must overcome when you read works written in previous centuries.

The first of these is language. Literary styles change from century to century (just as street language changes from decade to decade), and words come and go in mysterious ways. We all have a liking for the familiar, so there is a natural inclination to stick to contemporary fiction. But we cut ourselves off from a whole world of pleasure when we do this.

When reading an eighteenth- or nineteenth-century novel, it is important to accept the more leisurely pace both in the style and the plot. There are exceptions, of course, but in general you will find that the sentences may be longer, the nouns more frequently modified, and the story line a bit more rambling. The language and the meanderings of plot in Charles Dickens' *Nicholas Nickleby* or Henry Fielding's *Tom Jones* reflect the notion that fiction is like a tale narrated out loud by an amiable story teller. If you accept this approach as a natural part of the historical period, you will be able to enter into the spirit of the fiction.

The customs and conventions of earlier centuries can also be distracting. There are significant differences between our own period and theirs in such areas as the relations between the sexes and attitudes toward social class. These are worth noting. But don't let such contrasts wall you off from the work as a whole. The formality of social relationships and the concern for "a good marriage" in Jane Austen's *Pride and Prejudice*, for example, are not the peculiar beliefs of the author. They are a part of the historical setting.

In addition to fiction written in previous centuries, there are contemporary novels and short stories which make use of historical settings. Such works are highly varied, and some are more literarily sophisticated than others. The term *historical novel* has overtones of popularized fiction because that is how many (though not all) of them have been written. Some are not far from a very simple form of entertainment called *costume gothics* or just *gothics* which combine adventure, romance, and very predictable characters. They are popular with the mass market and are consumed without much thought or reflection, rather like soap operas on television.

What concerns us here are those novels which draw on historical periods to provide fiction which is not only entertaining but rich in insight and suggestion as well. Often such novels make social statements and contain characters who are memorable. John Fowles' novel, *The French Lieutenant's Woman,* for example, is set in the nineteenth century and raises some interesting questions about the conventions of the time and the impact of new attitudes on the Victorian world. It also poses the fascinating question of why we in the twentieth century are sometimes drawn to that earlier period—as indeed the author himself was while writing the book.

E. L. Doctorow's *Ragtime* is another well-known example. It is a highly readable novel which focuses on the early 1900s in this country and makes use of such historical figures as Henry Ford, J. P. Morgan, and Sigmund Freud as well as entirely fictional characters.

Sometimes such novels are fictionalized treatments of actual events; an example is Truman Capote's chilling *In Cold Blood.* The tendency is to handle the factual material in a straightforward manner, but this is not always the case. Robert Coover's *The Public Burning,* for example, is a highly imaginative and even bizarre treatment of a historical incident. Here the trial and execution of Julius and Ethel Rosenberg are treated in a dream-like manner which includes long monologues by Uncle Sam himself! A history text provides the facts of the past, but a novel attempts to recreate the spirit of a time as well.

SOCIAL SETTING

In addition to place and time, fiction often makes use of a social setting. Some works focus on the very rich, some on the middle class, and others on the poor. Within each of these broad and general classifications are a great variety of national, ethnic, racial, and age groupings which provide authors with a whole network of attitudes and traditions. Although not all works of fiction are concerned with the social setting, some make it central.

"On the Road" by Langston Hughes is a story in which both class and race play central roles. In the very first paragraph we learn that the pro-tagonist is poor and the time is "during the depression." He is, of course, an individual, but he represents many of the unemployed during that grim period of American history, and in a broader sense he brings to mind the down-and-out of any period.

In the second paragraph we are told that Sargeant is a "big black man with snow on his face." I will return to the significance of this use of color in Chapter 14 on symbolic suggestion. But it is worth noting here that what seems like a casual part of the setting—the winter scene with snow every-where—is an essential part of the theme. This is a story in black and white.

The social setting is central in this story. A poor man is dealing with those in power. This concern is dramatized by other aspects of setting as well: the season (white snow and a black man), the time of day (night as a "dark time" of our history as well), and the geographic setting (in mid-America).

Longer stories and novels sometimes provide a contrast between op-posing social groups or cultures. The groups can be rich and poor, black and white, rural and urban. Or they may be more subtle divisions such as the established members of a community and newcomers. Such divisions can produce highly dramatic fiction.

EXAMINING THE SETTING

When you begin a short story or novel, be sure to look carefully at *where* the action takes place. How wide a focus is being used? Is it limited to a room, a house, or a store? Or does it make use of geographic areas such as a particular region, a city, or a state? As you continue reading, consider whether this physical setting is contributing to the theme.

At the same time, look at *when* the action takes place. The historical period will probably be your first concern since this will have an immediate bearing on how you read the work; but don't forget the importance of the season and the time of day. As we saw in "On the Road," these can all take on a special significance.

Finally, take a close look at *who* these characters are in terms of social setting. This will not always be a major factor, but in some cases it will be central, as in "On the Road."

TOPICS FOR ANALYSIS

Here are some topics to consider for a class discussion or as the basis for short papers.

1.   Describe the apartment of Bill and Elizabeth Bailey in "The Sojourner." Since the author uses few details, you will have to invent them. In a concluding paragraph, explain briefly what evidence from the story directed your choices.

2.   Rewrite the first two paragraphs of "On The Road," converting the cold winter night to an oppressively hot summer day. Try to maintain as much of the original feeling as possible. Then explain briefly what kinds of problems you had in this conversion.

3.   Select two short stories from an anthology or two novels. Photocopy (or copy) the first half page from each. Underline the words and phrases which give you some notion of what the setting is. Then analyze the author's method of establishing the setting. Is it direct (a block of description) or indirect and fragmentary? Which work gives you the clearest picture in that initial half page?

It is not necessary to write papers on everything you read. It is not even necessary to subject every story and novel to a group discussion. One of the great pleasures in reading is simply getting lost in the material and not analyzing. But if you stop and look closely at aspects like setting in specific works from time to time, your mind will become sensitized to aspects of literature you might not have considered before. The time and effort you invest in close analysis—whether on your own or in a class—will give you heightened pleasure in all your future reading.

chapter 6

A & P

a story by John Updike

In walks these three girls in nothing but bathing suits. I'm in the third checkout slot, with my back to the door, so I don't see them until they're over by the bread. The one that caught my eye first was the one in the plaid green two-piece. She was a chunky kid, with a good tan and a sweet broad soft-looking can with those two crescents of white just under it, where the sun never seems to hit, at the top of the backs of her legs. I stood there with my hand on a box of HiHo crackers trying to remember if I rang it up or not. I ring it up again and the customer starts giving me hell. She's one of these cash-register-watchers, a witch about fifty with rouge on her cheekbones and no eyebrows, and I know it made her day to trip me up. She'd been watching cash registers for fifty years and probably never seen a mistake before.

By the time I got her feathers smoothed and her goodies into a bag—she gives me a little snort in passing, if she'd been born at the right time they would have burned her over in Salem—by the time I get her on her way the girls had circled around the bread and were coming back, without a pushcart, back my way along the counters, in the aisle between the checkouts and the Special bins. They didn't even have shoes on. There was this chunky one, with the two-piece—it was bright green and the seams on the bra were still sharp and her belly was still pretty pale so I guessed she just got it (the suit)—there was this one, with one of those chubby berry-faces, the lips all bunched together under her nose, this one, and a tall one, with black hair that hadn't quite frizzed right, and one of these sunburns right across under the eyes, and a chin that was too long— you know, the kind of girl other girls think is very "striking" and "attractive" but never quite makes it, as they very well know, which is why they like her so much—and then the third one, that wasn't quite so tall. She was the queen. She kind of led them, the other two peeking around and making their shoulders round. She didn't look around, not this queen, she just walked straight on slowly, on these long white primadonna legs. She came down a little hard on her heels, as if she didn't walk in bare feet that much, putting down her heels and then letting the weight move along to her toes as if she was testing the floor with every step, putting a little deliberate extra action into it. You never know for sure how girls' minds work (do you really think it's a mind in there or just a little buzz like a bee in a glass jar?) but you got the idea she had talked the other two into coming in here with her, and now she was showing them how to do it, walk slow and hold yourself straight.

She had on a kind of dirty-pink—beige maybe, I don't know— bathing suit with a little nubble all over it and, what got me, the straps were down. They were off her shoulders looped loose around the cool tops of her arms, and I guess as a result the suit had slipped a little on her, so all around the top of the cloth there was this shining rim. If it hadn't been there you wouldn't have known there could have been anything whiter than those shoulders. With the straps pushed off, there was nothing between the top of the suit and the top of her head except for just *her*, this clean bare plane of the top of her chest down from the shoulder bones like a dented sheet of metal tilted in the light. I mean, it was more than pretty.

She had a sort of oaky hair that the sun and salt had bleached, done up in a bun that was unravelling, and a kind of prim face. Walking into the A & P with your straps down, I suppose it's the only kind of face you *can* have. She held her head so high her neck, coming up out of those white shoulders, looked kind of stretched, but I didn't mind. The longer her neck was, the more of her there was.

She must have felt in the corner of her eye me and over my shoulder Stokesie in the second slot watching, but she didn't tip. Not this queen. She kept her eyes moving across the racks, and stopped, and turned so slow it made my stomach rub the inside of my apron, and buzzed to the other two, who kind of huddled against her for relief, and then they all three of them went up the cat-and-dog-food-breakfast-cereal-macaroni-rice-raisins-seasonings-spreads-spaghetti-soft-drinks-crackers-and-cookies aisle. From the third slot I look straight up this aisle to the meat counter, and I watched them all the way. The fat one with the tan sort of fumbled with the cookies, but on second thought she put the package back. The sheep pushing their carts down the aisle—the girls were walking against the usual traffic (not that we have one-way signs or anything)—were pretty hilarious. You could see them, when Queenie's white shoulders dawned on them, kind of jerk, or hop, or hiccup, but their eyes snapped back to their own baskets and on they pushed. I bet you could set off dynamite in an A & P and the people would by and large keep reaching and checking oatmeal off their lists and muttering "Let me see, there was a third thing, began with A, asparagus, no, ah, yes, applesauce!" or whatever it is they do mutter. But there was no doubt, this jiggled them. A few houseslaves in pin curlers even looked around after pushing their carts past to make sure what they had seen was correct.

You know, it's one thing to have a girl in a bathing suit down on the beach, where what with the glare nobody can look at each other much anyway, and another thing in the cool of the A & P, under the fluorescent lights, against all those stacked packages, with her feet paddling along naked over our checker-board green-and-cream rubber-tile floor.

"Oh Daddy," Stokesie said beside me. "I feel so faint."

"Darling," I said. "Hold me tight." Stokesie's married, with two babies chalked up on his fuselage already, but as far as I can tell that's the only difference. He's twenty-two, and I was nineteen this April.

"Is it done?" he asks, the responsible married man finding his voice. I forgot to say he thinks he's going to be manager some sunny day, maybe in 1990 when it's called the Great Alexandrov and Petrooshki Tea Company or something.

What he meant was, our town is five miles from a beach, with a big summer colony out on the Point, but we're right in the middle of town, and the women generally put on a shirt or shorts or something before they get out of the car into the street. And anyway these are usually women with six children and varicose veins mapping their legs and nobody, including them, could care less. As I say, we're right in the middle of town, and if you stand at our front doors you can see two banks and the Congregational church and the newspaper store and three real-estate offices and about twenty-seven old freeloaders tearing up Central Street because the sewer broke again. It's not as if we're on the Cape; we're north of Boston and there's people in this town haven't seen the ocean for twenty years.

The girls had reached the meat counter and were asking McMahon something. He pointed, they pointed, and they shuffled out of sight behind a pyramid of Diet Delight peaches. All that was left for us to see was old McMahon patting his mouth and looking after them sizing up their joints. Poor kids, I began to feel sorry for them, they couldn't help it.

Now here comes the sad part of the story, at least my family says it's sad, but I don't think it's so sad myself. The store's pretty empty, it being Thursday afternoon, so there was nothing much to do except lean on the register and wait for the girls to show up again. The whole store was like a pinball machine and I didn't know which tunnel they'd come out of. After a while they come around out of the far aisle, around the light bulbs, records at discount of the Caribbean Six or Tony Martin Sings or some such gunk you wonder they waste the wax on, six-packs of candy bars, and plastic toys done up in cellophane that fall apart when a kid looks at them anyway. Around they come, Queenie still leading the way, and holding a little gray jar in her hand. Slots Three through Seven are unmanned and I could see her wondering between Stokes and me, but Stokesie with his usual luck draws an old party in baggy gray pants who stumbles up with four giant cans of pineapple juice (what do these bums *do* with all that pineapple juice? I've often asked myself) so the girls come to me. Queenie puts down the jar and I take it into my fingers icy cold. Kingfish Fancy Herring Snacks in Pure Sour Cream: 49¢. Now her hands are empty, not a ring or a bracelet, bare as God made them, and I wonder where the money's coming from. Still with that prim look she lifts a folded dollar bill out of the hollow at the center of her nubbled pink top. The jar went heavy in my hand. Really, I thought that was so cute.

Then everybody's luck begins to run out. Lengel comes in from haggling with a truck full of cabbages on the lot and is about to scuttle into the door marked MANAGER behind which he hides all day when the girls touch his eye. Lengel's pretty dreary, teaches Sunday school and the rest, but he doesn't miss that much. He comes over and says, "Girls, this isn't the beach."

Queenie blushes, though maybe it's just a brush of sunburn I was noticing for the first time, now that she was so close. "My mother asked me to pick up a jar of herring snacks." Her voice kind of startled me, the way voices do when you see the people first, coming out so flat and dumb yet kind of tony, too, the way it ticked over "pick up" and "snacks." All of a sudden I slid right down her voice into her living room. Her father and the other men were standing around in ice-cream coats and bow ties and the women were in sandals picking up herring snacks on toothpicks off a big glass plate and they were all holding drinks the color of water with olives and sprigs of mint in them. When my parents have somebody over they get lemonade and if it's a real racy affair Schlitz in tall glasses with "They'll Do It Every Time" cartoons stencilled on.

"That's all right," Lengel said. "But this isn't the beach." His repeating this struck me as funny, as if it had just occurred to him, and he had been thinking all these years the A & P was a great big dune and he was the head lifeguard. He didn't like my smiling—as I say he doesn't miss much—but he concentrates on giving the girls that sad Sunday-school-superintendent stare.

Queenie's blush is no sunburn now, and the plump one in plaid, that I liked better from the back—a really sweet can—pipes up, "We weren't doing any shopping. We just came in for the one thing."

"That makes no difference," Lengel tells her, and I could see from the way his eyes went that he hadn't noticed she was wearing a two-piece before. "We want you decently dressed when you come in here."

"We *are* decent," Queenie says suddenly, her lower lip pushing, getting sore now that she remembers her place, a place from which the crowd that runs the A & P must look pretty crummy. Fancy Herring Snacks flashed in her very blue eyes.

"Girls, I don't want to argue with you. After this come in here with your shoulders covered. It's our policy." He turns his back. That's policy for you. Policy is what the kingpins want. What the others want is juvenile delinquency.

All this time, the customers had been showing up with their carts but, you know, sheep, seeing a scene, they had all bunched up on Stokesie, who shook open a paper bag as gently as peeling a peach, not wanting to miss a word. I could feel in the silence everybody getting nervous, most of all Lengel, who asks me, "Sammy, have you rung up their purchase?"

I thought and said "No" but it wasn't about that I was thinking. I go through the punches, 4, 9, GROC, TOT—it's more complicated than you think, and after you do it often enough, it begins to make a little song, that you hear words to, in my case "Hello (*bing*) there, you (*gung*) hap-py *pee*-pul (*splat*)!"—the *splat* being the drawer flying out. I uncrease the bill, tenderly as you may imagine, it just having come from between the two smoothest scoops of vanilla I had ever known there were, and pass a half and a penny into her narrow pink palm, and nestle the herrings in a bag and twist its neck and hand it over, all the time thinking.

The girls, and who'd blame them, are in a hurry to get out, so I say "I quit" to Lengel quick enough for them to hear, hoping they'll stop and watch me, their unsuspected hero. They keep right on going, into the electric eye; the door flies open and they flicker across the lot to their car, Queenie and Plaid and Big Tall Goony-Goony (not that as raw material she was so bad), leaving me with Lengel and a kink in his eyebrow.

"Did you say something, Sammy?"

"I said I quit."

"I thought you did."

"You didn't have to embarrass them."

"It was they who were embarrassing us."

I started out to say something that came out "Fiddle-de-do." It's a saying of my grandmother's, and I know she would have been pleased.

"I don't think you know what you're saying," Lengel said.

"I know you don't," I said. "But I do." I pull the bow at the back of my apron and start shrugging it off my shoulders. A couple of customers that had been heading for my slot begin to knock against each other, like scared pigs in a chute.

Lengel sighs and begins to look very patient and old and gray. He's been a friend of my parents for years. "Sammy, you don't want to do this to your Mom and Dad," he tells me. It's true, I don't. But it seems to me that once you begin a gesture it's fatal not to go through with it. I fold the apron, "Sammy" stitched in red on the pocket, and put it on the counter, and drop the bow tie on top of it. The bow tie is theirs, if you've ever wondered. "You'll feel this for the rest of your life," Lengel says, and I know that's true, too, but remembering how he made that pretty girl blush makes me so scrunchy inside I punch the No Sale tab and the machine whirs "pee-pul" and the drawer splats out. One advantage to this scene taking place in summer, I can follow this up with a clean exit, there's no fumbling around getting your coat and galoshes, I just saunter into the electric eye in my white shirt that my mother ironed the night before, and the door heaves itself open, and outside the sunshine is skating around on the asphalt.

I look around for my girls, but they're gone, of course. There wasn't anybody but some young married screaming with her children about some candy they didn't get by the door of a powder-blue Falcon station wagon. Looking back in the big windows, over the bags of peat moss and aluminum lawn furniture stacked on the pavement, I could see Lengel in my place in the slot, checking the sheep through. His face was dark gray and his back stiff, as if he's just had an injection of iron, and my stomach kind of fell as I felt how hard the world was going to be to me hereafter.

chapter 7

POINT OF VIEW

first-person fiction
third-person fiction
point of view (the means of
* perception): single, multiple*
* omniscient, limited omniscient*
the range of choices
topics for analysis

Point of view brings us back to one of the five basic questions posed in Chapter 1: "How is this work of fiction being told?" More precisely, we should ask "How and by whom?" The "how" is referred to as *person* (first person, "I," or third person, "he" or "she"), and the "by whom" is *point of view* (through whose eyes are we seeing this fictional scene?). Every story ever told or written is shaped by these two sets of alternatives.

FIRST-PERSON FICTION

When we use the first person, "I," in conversation, our listeners assume we are talking about ourselves. This same form lends itself to fiction naturally. But there is a significant difference: When an author writes a story or novel in the first person, the "speaker" is a fictional character. Authors do often write about themselves factually, but when they do the result is called *autobiography* and is not considered fiction at all. Fiction is by definition based on imaginary characters—including the narrator.

We are all aware of this distinction between fiction and factual writing, but there is still an inclination to think of stories and novels written in the first person as probably being closer to the author's own experience than those written in the third person. Actually the reverse is true in many cases. Authors who draw heavily on personal experience frequently disguise their own involvement by writing in the third person. In the same way, some well-known first-person novels are "told" by a central character far removed from the author. For this reason it is a mistake to suggest that an author believes something simply because of what his or her fictional narrator has said.

To avoid confusion, the fictional character who tells a story in the first person is referred to as the *persona* or *narrator*. In fiction, the two terms are essentially the same, so I will use the more familiar *narrator*. In John Updike's story, "A & P," for example, Sammy is the fictional narrator. He is partially aware of the significance of his experience in the supermarket, but as I will explain shortly, his view is neither as broad nor as deep as the author's.

Once you are a third of the way into a story or novel told in the first person, ask yourself whether the narrator is being handled in a sympathetic manner or is to some degree being satirized. There is no sharp division between the two, so think of them as gradations on a scale. At one end of the spectrum, we share the thoughts and feelings of such characters and identify ourselves with them. At the other, we view these characters more from the outside, smiling at or perhaps disapproving of them.

It is not always easy to be sure just what attitude the author is taking toward a first-person narrator—particularly at first. But usually you can tell from the tone of the writing. Read the following two paragraphs, imagining each to be the opening of a story:

(A)

I've been out of school three years, and so far I haven't had much luck with jobs. I've had five and none of them worked out. One trouble is that I get bored with routine work, and then I'm apt to say something I don't mean. That gets me into trouble. Last week was a good example.

(B)

I've been out of school three years and I've learned one thing—those that hire sure love to fire. Anyone who gets to be boss is just naturally sadistic. They take pleasure in making it tough for those under them. I ought to know. I've been fired for no reason whatever five times already. Last week was the worst so far.

In the first paragraph we seem to be dealing with a narrator who has a problem but is willing to look at it in a reasonable way. There is no suggestion that the author intends to ridicule the character.

With the second, however, we have the feeling that the author is ridiculing the speaker right from the start. Part of this feeling is based on the fact that the character (not the author) tends to blame others for what is probably his or her own fault. Having five "sadistic" bosses, after all, seems just a bit unlikely. Already we know something about the narrator that he or she won't admit. This establishes a kind of distance between us and the character. As the story develops, we will keep looking for other clues about the narrator's problem, but we won't trust his or her own interpretation. Characters like this are called *unreliable narrators* because we cannot trust their opinions. Unreliable narrators are quite often the subjects of satire in fiction.

How can we be sure a character is being satirized? A good deal depends on the degree of exaggeration. This is a matter of tone, which is the subject of Chapter 13. There is never any doubt about extreme satire because the characters are almost like cartoons. When George Orwell presents the leadership of the Soviet Union as a group of scheming pigs (in *Animal Farm*) we know exactly where he stands! But what about John Updike's attitude toward his narrator in "A & P"? On the one hand, Sammy can be described as a rather foolish individual to lose his job in a futile gesture regarding three young women he has never met. But there is something admirable about his stand too. There are gently satiric elements in this story, but the author respects his narrator.

Tone, then, is an important element to consider when determining whether a narrator is being treated satirically. But tone depends to some degree on individual interpretation and for this reason is occasionally difficult to prove. Internal inconsistencies are another indication that a character is being satirized, and these are sometimes blatant. If a narrator says he is pursued by women and clearly isn't, that tells us something he is not willing to admit. Or a character may say she is kind or generous and then show by her actions that she is not. These are good indications that the character is being treated to some degree satirically.

The general principle to keep in mind is this: Regardless of whether the first-person narrator is presented sympathetically or is being ridiculed, remember that he or she is a fictional creation. Judge that character carefully, weighing actions as well as words.

Another significant variation in first-person fiction is the degree to which the style echoes spoken language. A majority of first-person stories and novels use language which is similar to what we are used to seeing in nonfiction. This is called a *neutral style*. It is "neutral" in that it is neither as formal as academic papers usually are nor is it as colloquial as spoken language.

Some first-person fiction, on the other hand, is written in a style which intentionally echoes informal speech. It makes use of both informal phrasing and slang. This is called *as-if-spoken* or *colloquial style*. Here are three versions of the same passage which illustrate the spectrum between neutral first-person fiction and the more informal or colloquial approach:

(A)

I don't think much of stock-car racing. First of all, the spectators park all over my fields. And then there's the sound and the smell of the contestants. My guess is that half the crowd is too intoxicated to tell one entry from another.

(B)

I don't take to that there stock-car racing. All those folks parking on my fields. The roar and the stink of all those cars. Half the crowd's too drunk to know who's winning anyway.

(C)

I don't cotton to them auto races. All them hoodlums parked every whichway over my fields, all that ruckus and stink, the crowd too boozed to tell one of them ugly buggers from another.

Although all of these are in the first person, *A* is closer to the neutral style we are used to in the third person. The sentences are complete and none contain colloquial expressions. This is by far the most common approach in fiction.

The second version makes minor changes in wording: "spectators" become "folks," for example, and "sound and smell" become "roar and stink." Also the connectives in the first version ("First of all," and "then") disappear in the more informal second passage.

The third relies heavily on phrasing associated with very informal speech. There are four words and phrases generally considered to be slang. The use of "them" is also strictly colloquial. Although widely heard, it would be considered an error in written English. The passage does not use phonetic spelling (contemporary fiction rarely does that), but it has the unmistakable flavor of common speech.

The as-if-spoken style is rare in short stories and still more unusual in novels. One reason for this may be that unfamiliar phrasing and especially altered spelling can make fiction more difficult to read. Much depends on the degree of variation from standard written English. If you would like to see some examples, look up some of these works: "Why I Live at the P.O.," a short story by Eudora Welty (Southern white dialect); *Their Eyes Were Watching God*, a novel by Zora Neale Hurston (Southern black dialect); *One Flew Over the Cuckoo's Nest* by Ken Kesey (the voice of an urbanized American Indian). These are all highly successful examples of a little-used approach.

Closely related to the as-if-told style is an approach which might be called *as-if-thought*. This style is generally referred to as *stream-of-consciousness writing*. The illusion is often created with run-on sentences and an apparently random sequence of ideas and impressions which is based more on free association than on logical order. There is a famous example of stream-of-consciousness writing at the end of James Joyce's *Ulysses*. More recent samples are found in sections of Robert Coover's impressionistic novel, *The Public Burning*. Most authors use the technique sparingly and in short passages rather than as the basis of an entire novel.

The narrator of a story or novel written in the first person is usually the central character or protagonist. But not necessarily. Sometimes the narrator is a secondary or even a minor character who is in a position to observe the central events of a work. One advantage of this approach is that the author is able to withhold information from the reader, limiting our view just as it is so frequently limited in our daily lives.

THIRD-PERSON FICTION

The third person is used far more frequently than the first person. Short-story anthologies often include five or six third-person selections for every one in the first person. The ratio in contemporary novels is almost the same.

There are two mechanical advantages to writing in the third person. The first is that it provides a more natural ending for those works in which the protagonist dies. It also provides a way to describe the central character. Amateur writers (and some professionals too) occasionally have their protagonists stand in front of a mirror and reflect on themselves: "The image which stared back at me was short, pudgy, almost pig-like." That will do, but having first-person narrators staring into mirrors can seem like a rather obvious technique, and it can't be used to show much more than physical characteristics.

The most important advantage of the third person, however, is flexibility. Authors can, if they wish, shift from the mind of one character to another and, in addition, present information directly. Such freedoms are used sparingly in contemporary fiction, but both techniques are enormously valuable. In order to understand the popularity of third-person writing, we have to examine these two ways of shifting the *point of view*.

POINT OF VIEW

In daily conversation we use *point of view* to mean someone's opinion or attitude. We say, "From her point of view, education is a major priority." When applied to fiction, however, the term is more precise. It refers to the character through whose eyes a piece of fiction appears to be presented. For example, "The Sojourner" is written from John Ferris' point of view. Point of view is also called the *means of perception*, a phrase which is more

of communicating the information than having a sentence like, "Suddenly it struck him that he was thirty-eight" or, as direct thought, "Here I am, thirty-eight and still not settled down."

Langston Hughes also presents almost all of "On the Road" through the eyes of his protagonist, but there is a touch of the author's voice in this passage:

> And down among the trees and bushes there were makeshift houses made out of boxes and tin and old pieces of wood and canvas. You couldn't see them in the dark, but you knew they were there if you'd ever been on the road, if you had ever lived with the homeless and hungry in a depression.

Authors are presumably *omniscient* about their own work—that is, they know everything about their characters and the outcome of the plot. But even though they occasionally reveal their presence at least subtly, they unfold most of their fiction through the eyes of a particular character. This mixed viewpoint is called *limited omniscience*. The term helps us to see how an author knowingly withholds his or her own knowledge and opinions to help give us the feeling that we are entering the fiction directly, learning about the situation through one of the characters.

In the eighteenth and nineteenth centuries, the approach to fiction was slightly different. It was common practice for novelists to enter their works frequently not only to fill in background information but to comment on the characters and even on the way the story was developing. For example, in his novel *Vanity Fair,* William Thackeray dispenses with one aspect of his plot with the statement, "We are not going to write the history; it would be too dreary and stupid." And at another point, "Let us skip over the interval in the history of her downward progress." This kind of comment is referred to as the *authorial voice.*

When you read novels that use this device, resist the temptation to think of them as "old-fashioned." Imagine yourself listening to a skilled story teller narrating a lengthy anecdote. Many of these writers thought of themselves in just this way. It was entirely natural for them to address their readers as if they were physically present. You will enjoy such work far more if you listen for the author's "voice" in the style. This will help you to accept the more leisurely pace and occasional digression.

Although few authors today enter their fiction directly in this way, some have made dramatic or comic use of the authorial voice. It can have a special effect simply because we are not used to it. If this approach interests you, here are three examples, all available in paperback and in most libraries: John Fowles' *The French Lieutenant's Woman,* Margaret Drabble's *The Middle Ground,* and several works by John Barth including the title story in a collection called *Lost in the Funhouse.*

THE RANGE OF CHOICES

Since there is a great variety in the ways writers of fiction handle viewpoint, think of them as forming a spectrum. It begins with work which is strictly limited to the thoughts within the mind of a single character and moves in stages to fiction in which the means of perception is distributed among different characters and is shared with an omniscient author as well.

- Stream-of-consciousness writing (a monologue entirely within the mind of a character):

A bad decision living way out here. Too isolated. I'm not a country person. Not used to it. This place is nowhere. The boonies. . . .

- First person colloquial or as-if-told (a monologue written as if spoken out loud—sometimes with quotation marks but more often without):

Well, to be honest, it wasn't such a good idea moving way out here. Too darn isolated for one thing. And I'm not a country person, you know. This is really the boonies.

- First-person neutral style:

It wasn't a good idea moving out here. It's too isolated for one thing. And I'm not a country person. This is miles from anywhere.

- Third person with a single means of perception.

He regretted moving out there. It was too isolated for him. And he hadn't been raised in the country. The place was miles from any town.

- Third person with a double means of perception:

He regretted moving out there. It was too isolated for him. He brooded about it a lot and complained to his wife. But she just smiled and nodded. She knew it was the best thing that had happened to him in years.

- Third person with a double means of perception and a single sentence (the final one) from the author's point of view:

He regretted moving out there. It was too isolated for him. He brooded about it a lot and complained to his wife. She just smiled and nodded. She knew it was the best thing that had happened to him in years. But in three weeks she would discover she was pregnant, and that would mark the end of their stay in the country.

- Third-person omniscient style (note the shifting means of perception and the frequent intrusions by the author):

He regretted moving out there. Like so many city dwellers who become addicted to constant sociability, he thought it was too isolated for him. He complained to his wife, but the poor woman had romantic notions about country living. She had convinced herself that it was good for him, though in fact she was motivated more by her own needs. In three weeks, however, she would discover she was pregnant. That would mark the end of their stay in the country but also the beginning of our story.

TOPICS FOR ANALYSIS

One of the best ways to get to know a story or novel really well is to study the point of view. You can do this informally, considering some of the following topics and working them through in your own mind. Or, for a more thorough treatment, you can use one of them as the basis of a short paper.

1. Select a first-person story or novel which is written in as-if-spoken style. ("A & P" is a good example. Three other possible titles were suggested on page 51.) Analyze how the illusion of speech is achieved. Try to be as specific as you can, listing some of the words and phrases which give the flavor of spoken language. Has the author used spelling variations or merely appropriate phrasing? How about sentence structure?

2. Rewrite the opening paragraph of "On The Road" and the *second* paragraph of "The Sojourner," converting each from third-person writing to first. Try to capture the flavor of speech each man might use. You may find that this requires more than merely replacing "he" with "I." When you are through, analyze some of the choices you made to achieve this effect.

3. Review a story or novel which is written in the third person and make a list of phrases and sentences which come from the author directly. (Any work will do, but fiction previous to our own century will contain more examples.) Do they reveal important aspects of the theme, or are they mainly intended to provide background information? How might the author have shown the same information through action or dialogue?

4. Select two stories (or short scenes from novels) which represent two different approaches in the scale outlined on page 56. Briefly analyze the means of perception in each work and photocopy a paragraph which illustrates your analysis. Then rewrite each paragraph using the type of viewpoint adopted by the other author—that is, convert each paragraph to the other approach. This is not as difficult as you might imagine, and you will learn a good deal from it.

5. Select a story or novel which is presented in the third person from a single point of view. ("The Sojourner" would be a good choice, but any story with several characters will do.) Analyze what changes would occur if the means of perception were shifted to another character in that same work. Would the reader learn different things? Would the shift in emphasis change the theme?

Whether you plan to write a paper or not, always look closely at the point of view in each story or novel you read. If you do this as you begin, you will see how important it is in the development of character, plot, suspense—indeed, every aspect of the work.

chapter 8

SMALL POINT BRIDGE

a story by Stephen Minot

It was March 31 and Isaac Bates had survived still another Maine winter. Now, his solitary lunch finished, he stood for a moment by the large living-room window and looked down over the white stubble of glazed brush, farther down to the ledges along the shore and out to the churning sea, and enjoyed his one cigar for the day. He also savored their consternation: sons and daughters in Connecticut, Tennessee, California, and all over, neighbors back on the town road, all amazed that a man of seventy who could easily afford to live anywhere would stick it out for the length of another winter. He had been snowed in for two months and three days. The old dirt road between his place and the highway was too steep for truck or tractor plowing; and even now, with the partial thaw, it was only fit for Jeep travel. There weren't many who would put up with all of that.

"No *sir*," he said aloud.

It hadn't been easy. It never was, of course, but this year the snows had come early and the oil truck couldn't make a December delivery so by January he was using the kerosene space heater and by February he was back to coal in the cookstove and wood in the fireplaces. The children were forever writing him to get out of there; but what the hell, generations had lived in that house on the heat of good oak firewood. Better for you anyway. Oil heat cakes the lungs.

So now he was almost up to another April. During the dark months he'd told himself that if he stuck it to April he'd last another year and, as he told the children, a man of seventy has to bargain for short-term leases. The low point had come when the pipes froze and he had to shut off the water. That meant shoveling a path to the outhouse. In the old days he and the boys kept that path open morning by morning which was easier in the long run than cutting through three-months accumulation . . . . Well, that was all behind him now.

But the winter wasn't through yet. There was still a kick to it. A March gale had begun the previous day and had built up strong during the night. Now, spitting sleet and rain, it churned the bay into an ugly froth. Only a month ago the ice had been thick enough for deer to wander out to the islands, and one young fool had driven his Ford pick-up out past Peniel Island just for the dare of it. But now the gale had broken that white valley up into slabs of forty and fifty tons and was grinding them against the shore. Tide and wind had jacked them up into weird angles like a nightmare of train wrecks. But unlike boxcars, they were forever moving—slow as a clock's hand and with a force you could hardly believe.

There was one year when the ice had caught hold of the marine railway he used to haul his fishing boats. Within an agonizing week it had pried those railroad tracks from the ties spike by spike and had slowly twisted them into hairpin shapes. The memory of it made him grimace even now.

From where he stood in his living room he could hear the inhuman whine and grunt as ice heaved blindly against ledge. The sound had been loud enough to pry its way into his dreams the night before.

"Snarl all you want," he muttered, and blew cigar smoke against the window where it broke like surf. "You can't move granite." His shore line was solid ledge, and there was satisfaction in that. It was solid like his house, like the plate glass that stood between him and the driving sleet—he had seen full-grown pheasants break their necks against that glass.

The storm would do damage at the cannery. He knew that. He had seen the ice lock onto the base of a pile two feet thick and work it back and forth with the incoming tide, pulling it clear out of the muck and lifting the pier above it as well. He'd seen the oak hull of a lobster boat crushed like a beer can in a young man's grip. No sir, he wouldn't get by a winter like this without getting hurt somewhere. But there was money for repairs. In half a century he had built his cannery with solid blocks of effort: first, fresh crabmeat for the summer hotels; then canned crabmeat statewide; finally frozen seafood of all types coast to coast. As his billboards said, "You Can't Beat Bates for Frozen Fishcakes." And no one had. No matter what they threw at him, there was always the satisfaction that he had insured himself with bank accounts. "There's more than one way to build a sea wall," he said, and nodded, serving as his own audience.

But he was talking to himself again. That wasn't good. It meant he was getting weak-headed. "Keep your mouth shut," he said. What he needed was a little activity.

Then he remembered that this was the 31st. This was the day he had to see Seth. He probably should have taken care of it before this, but now they were at the deadline. And he had almost forgotten it.

It was a small business matter and Seth would be surprised that such details are important—Seth being a simple man. But a debt's a debt and all the world knew that. If you let the little things go—well, it's like not tending to a small leak.

"Rotten day to be out," he said, but he felt no deep resentment. He never expected the weather to give him an even break.

He went to the front hall and began burrowing in the cluttered closet. "Where's those boots?" he muttered. "Damn it, Ella, where's those boots?" Then he clamped his jaw on his cigar, cursing himself silently. Ella was dead—dead, buried, and gone two years now. It was weak-headed to call her name. Besides, it wouldn't do to let her know he was still living here. "Promise," she said, looking up at him from that ugly hospital bed, and he had promised: he would move out of the old place when she was gone. And he would, too—when the time came to join her.

"Where the hell . . . ?" And he spotted his boots just where he had left them on the chair—together with his coat, his lumberman's cap, his tool box, his axe, his snow shovel, the broken car jack, his extra set of chains, and an empty antifreeze can. Of course. "Got to clean up this goddamn mess," he said with the tone he used to use on the children.

The old barn was dank and colder than the outside air; but for all this his Jeep started easily enough. During the winter months Isaac had run the motor for an hour each week with religious regularity; that, plus the recent trips to the store, had left the battery charged. All it took was a little foresight.

He backed out and drove past the barn through the apple orchards and down into the spruce grove. At the bottom of the ravine by the brook he stopped and shifted into four-wheel drive. The long, twisting ascent was a brutal challenge. It took two wild runs, wheels whining and spewing half-frozen cakes of mud; but he made it, finally, with a grunt of satisfaction.

"Crazy road," he muttered to himself, as he had said to every visitor who had ever come over it. It was the only route out from the farm to the highway and thus the only link with the store, with the town, and even with his cannery. He had cursed it and repaired it every spring; but it had its uses. It moved the assessors to pity, kept salesmen out, turned back summer tourists, and intimidated talkative neighbors. There was no gate or sign that could do all that.

Once on the tar road, he made good time. He had to dodge fallen branches and allow for sleet on the pavement, but it was not long before he came to the turn which led back onto his own acreage again, back down to the sea again where his cannery stood gray and silent on ice-caked piles, dormant and waiting like his orchard.

Small Point Road ran parallel to the sea from the cannery to Seth's place, less than a quarter-mile. It was a godforsaken bit of coastline with a few unpainted houses, a dump, and only scrub oak and choke cherry for coverage.

Isaac owned that entire section of the coast including Small Point itself, a useless nob of land cut off from the shore by muck at low tide and six feet of water at high. Seth had built his house out there with permission. It was made from driftwood and used lumber collected over the years he had spent working at the cannery. It didn't look like much—just a wood-shingled shack actually—but you could see it was put together with care. None of the windows matched, for example, but they were well fitted and puttied and not a cracked pane in the lot.

He had also built the ramshackle footbridge which led out to the house. As Isaac started to walk across it he could feel the ice heave against the untrimmed spruce piling. The cold wind seared his lungs and made his eyes tear and he wondered what drove a man to live like this. He hung on to the railing as if it were a lifeline and watched his footing carefully. Sections of the footbridge were already out of alignment, leaving gaps and twisting the planks.

"Goddamned thing ought to be condemned," Isaac muttered. But he forgot all that when his feet touched solid ground again. "Ah!" he said, and headed for the shack.

Seth opened the door even before the knock. His eyesight had grown poor and at first he only squinted, not recognizing Isaac. Then he nodded as if he had known all along. Isaac stepped in quickly and shut the door against the wind.

"Just having breakfast," Seth said. As night watchman, his day began in the afternoon. He was a short man and stooped, so he had to peer up at Isaac when he spoke. "Got some hot coffee going."

"It'll take more than coffee," Isaac said, struggling with his boots.

"I've got some of that too."

"Just a thimble, Seth. Can't stay long."

It was a one-room place, furnished only with necessities: wood stove, kitchen table, two straight chairs, and a bunk of two-by-fours built against the wall. Along the opposite wall were hooks on which his clothes and foul-weather gear were hung neatly. It was all snug enough until you looked out the front window and saw the ominous blocks of ice shoved in a jumble up the ledge to within twenty feet of the house.

Seth poured coffee from the percolator on the stove and then got a fifth of King's Whiskey from a cupboard and added a liberal jigger. They sat down at the table.

"Hasn't let up much," Isaac said.

"She's got another night to run."

"Bad time for it," Isaac said. "One more week and we'd be free of that ice." They nodded. "That bridge of yours has heaved a bit."

"Always does."

"I don't suppose you'd consider staying ashore till this ice clears out?"

"I don't suppose," Seth said, closing the subject.

"How's the cannery pier?" Isaac asked.

"Well now, we've got some work to do there. One or two spiles are loose. Don't know just how much yet."

"If it's bad enough, we might raise it up a foot or so. Wouldn't do any harm."

"We could get more rock underneath. It's weight we need."

And they were off on a familiar topic. Seth had spent most of his life working at the cannery as general maintenance man and had finally shifted to watchman with reluctance; but his real asset to the plant was still as planner and adviser in the endless task of rebuilding the pier. And for a hobby he worked on his own footbridge. It was the best game he knew—a sustained and personalized conflict. When they survived a bad winter gale he would say "We got her licked that time"; and when the hurricane of 1954 smashed two sections of the pier and carried off the ice house as well he said "She sure as hell got us this time." That with a wry grin too.

So the two of them spent an hour, sipping spiked coffee and talking timbers and bracing, hardly hearing the gale outside.

But there was the business part of the meeting too, and Isaac had a mind for business.

"Say," he said at last, "there's a small matter I don't want to forget."

"What's that?"

"Well, you might call it rent."

There was a pause. The ice grinding against the ledge out front was now as clear as if someone had opened a door. The house shuddered a bit as a gust slammed by.

"I don't believe you've asked that before," Seth said at last, speaking slowly. "Seems like when I inquired about building out here, you just nodded. That was a time ago, of course."

"Twenty years this April first. Tomorrow."

"That's quite a memory for dates you have. And how much were you figuring I might owe you?"

"A dollar would do it, Seth."

"Dollar a year?"

"No, for the whole twenty." He finished his mug. "It's just a fluke of the law, Seth. Law says a man takes possession after twenty years unless he's renting." Seth didn't answer "What I mean is, if a man lives in a place for twenty years . . . ."

Seth raised his hand for silence. "You're not telling me anything." He went to the wall where there was a calendar advertising "Granite Farms Pure Milk and Cream." He lifted the March sheet and pointed to the date of April 1. It was circled in red crayon.

"You sure as hell caught me this time," he said. "You've got more of the bastard in you than most folks realize." This with a wry smile. But then the smile vanished and he sat down again.

He squinted at Isaac, though at that distance he could see perfectly well. Then a hesitant smile came over his face again and he said, "Ike, is this your idea of an April Fool's trick? We're gettin' a bit advanced for that . . . ."

"No trick," Isaac said. He hadn't expected the resistance—just a dollar, after all. "This here's my land."

"Well for Lord's sake." It was as if Seth had only just then believed it. "You're serious."

"It's only a dollar I'm talking about."

"You can talk blue—you're getting no dollar from me."

"If it's the money, Seth, I could lend it to you."

"And hold possession for another twenty years? I don't fancy that."

"Then I'll deduct it from your pay."

"You'll deduct nothing. Not without my say-so."

"I've got the law, Seth, clear and straight. The land's mine."

"I've got the law too, when it comes to that. If I'm still sitting here at midnight, this here point is mine outright. I'm telling you, I'm not leaving. Not without being dragged. And you're not the man for dragging even the likes of me."

"For God's sake!" Isaac stood up, caught without words. Seth hadn't moved; he just looked up with a face flushed red. Then Isaac said in a rush, "You must be getting weak-headed. One dollar! You want me to go to court for one damn dollar?"

"You can go straight to hell for a dollar."

Isaac seized his coat and struggled into it, trembling with silent fury. He flung the door open. The wind slapped his face. "You're crazy out of your mind," he said and slammed the door behind him.

He stood there a moment, his rage sending tremors through his entire body. What could you do with a man like that? What the hell would it take to budge him?

Then he noticed that the wind had swung into the east a bit. Some of the ice slabs were being shifted, heaving murderously against the cannery pilings. From where he stood he could see that one corner of the loading platform had been weakened and now sagged. A wooden barrel of sawdust had already been dumped into the jumble of ice. No matter. He knew there'd be damage.

Then like the wind his mind shifted into a new quarter. There was hope after all.

Abruptly he turned and pounded on the door. "Seth," he called out. "Seth!" And as the door opened: "The pier. The cannery pier. We've got to get stuff out of there before the whole thing goes."

Seth peered by him, eyes squinting. "Something's smashed already," he said. "Wait up."

He disappeared but reappeared again in an incredibly short time, dressed in foul weather gear and boots. "Hurry up," he said, surging ahead along the footbridge, lumbering awkwardly in his boots. Isaac kept step right behind him as if driving him on.

They were halfway across the bridge when Seth stopped dead. Isaac piled into him with a grunt of surprise. "Go on," he said roughly.

"I remembered. I just remembered." Seth was almost whining. "You can't . . . ."

Isaac didn't want to hear him. He just pushed, grunting. "Go on," he kept saying, "Go on. Move. Go on." He pried at Seth's hand which was locked onto the railing.

They heaved against each other, almost evenly matched, senseless in their rage. Then Isaac raised his hand high and brought the edge of it down hard on Seth's wrist like a cleaver.

That did it. A squeal, a falling back, and a great rumbling like a line of boxcars being suddenly nudged, the sound resounding against his chest. Isaac felt a deep surge of power and then, catching sight of something larger out of the corner of his eye, turned just in time to see the whole front wall of his cannery pier buckle and slide toward the saw-tooth jumble of gray ice.

The freight-car rumble continued as the wall was wrenched free, slowly as in films, so that he could now see right into those rooms where he had spent his life. The floor heaved forward and objects started sliding toward the sea: a mop, two cleaning buckets, chairs, now the stainless-steel vat—the new one—and the freezer itself was beginning to rip from its fastenings. Upstairs the parts room dumped whole shelves of nuts, bolts, small hardware and cases of empty cans on the ice like pepper; and there, incredibly, was his office and his old oak desk and swivel chair with green cushion sliding faster now with filing cabinets and then splintering down the back of a littered plank of ice. A file drawer split open like a flower-pot and the records of a lifetime flew like snow.

He neither moved nor spoke. It was outrageous. The brutality of it shocked him. It wasn't like other storms. There had been no contest. How was a man to fight back?

Then the bridge on which they were standing gave a sudden shudder.

"Seth!" he said, half in warning and half in fear. But Seth was clinging onto the railing and staring at the remains of the cannery with his mouth open. He was paralyzed. Isaac would have to act for them both.

He looked first toward the shore and then toward the island. The distance was equal. The planks under them lurched to a severe angle. He swung his arm around Seth and firmly guided him back out to his house.

By the time they were at the front door, the bridge behind them was on its side and going through slow convulsions.

"It too," Isaac muttered in disbelief. He held tighter to Seth as if they were still in immediate danger. Then he stumbled into the protection of the house and shut the door against all that brutality.

Inside, neither of them spoke. They sat there, panting, one on the bed and the other in a chair, staring at their own thoughts.

And why, Isaac asked himself, did I do a damn fool thing like that? If we were ashore now, I'd have broken his hold on this place easy as . . . .

Some great slab of gray ice in the twilight outside bellowed like a live thing—like Isaac himself when crossed. He shuddered and then tensed again as if reliving the crisis they had just passed through. Then he shook his head. Crazy thoughts, he muttered to himself, for a man my age.

"You're a hard, cold sonofabitch," Seth said, speaking slowly, staring at the floor. Isaac looked over at him sitting there on the edge of the bed. He was still in his foul weather gear, a crumpled pile of black rubber like something washed up after a storm . . . like bits and pieces from the wrecked cannery.

Alarm struck Isaac as unexpectedly as a slap of spray. Had he spent a lifetime on that miserable coast only to end up harsh as the sea itself?

"That's not so," he said sharply. "I brought you back out here, didn't I? The place will be yours."

"I don't want no gift."

"I don't take to giving."

"I've noticed."

"Fact is," Isaac said, thinking aloud now, "you wouldn't be worth a pile of rags if you were forced back into town."

"Nor would you." His voice was still no more than a mutter.

"Well, we'll get your bridge built again," Isaac said, lighting a kerosene lamp against the growing darkness. "Hell, I have to re-build my own road every spring. No different. And the cannery—I can get that rebuilt too. There's money."

"But is there time?" Seth said.

They looked at each other squarely, but they chose not to an-swer the question. Seth stood up, finally, and shrugged off his foul weather gear. Then he lit the other lamp.

Later that night, after supper together, they played cards and drank hot whiskey. And when the sounds of the ice occasionally broke through, Isaac sang ballads which he had known as a boy and which had lain dormant in him like seeds through the course of a long, hard winter.

chapter 9

NARRATIVE TENSIONS

narrative tension defined
types of dramatic conflict: person
against person, the group, force
of nature, self
dramatic questions (withheld
information): suspense and
surprise
examining tension
topics for analysis

NARRATIVE TENSION DEFINED

Narrative *tension* is the dramatic element in fiction which holds our attention and keeps us turning pages. It is the source of vitality in what we read. Often it takes the form of conflict between individuals or groups. But it can also be created through dramatic questions, suspense, surprise, and shock.

Fiction almost always contains some form of tension. Oddly, this is not true of other types of prose. In fact, a great deal of what we read is essentially static—factual reports, for example, many historical accounts, magazine articles, instructional documents, and textbooks. In most cases, that kind of writing holds our attention simply because it gives us the information or the analysis we need. Once that service has been provided, the document is of little interest to us except to refresh our memories.

Fiction often provides factual information too. We may learn a good deal about sailing from a Conrad story or life among rural black Americans from a novel by Zora Neale Hurston. But acquiring information is not the main reason we read stories and novels. The pleasure we draw from fiction comes largely from the illusion of experiencing events as if they were literally a part of our own lives. Tension is what holds us in that strange, suspended state.

TYPES OF DRAMATIC
CONFLICT

Almost every fictional narrative ever told or written contains some type of dramatic *conflict*—everything from African folk tales, Greek epics, and Arabian fables, to Victorian novels, and *New Yorker* stories.

Simple fiction makes use of dramatic conflict in very simple ways. The Western, a type of popular fiction which later became the pattern for countless films and, still later, television dramas, pits a hero against one or more villains. War stories set the "good guy" against the enemy in much the same way.

But don't let these associations cloud the fact that the struggle between individuals can be a subtle and complex element in sophisticated fiction. Take another look at the dramatic structure of John Updike's story "A & P." No one hits anyone in that story, but the conflict between the protagonist, Sammy, and the manager of the store, Lengel, is central. On the most obvious level, it is a rather comic dispute which causes Sammy to lose his first job. But on a more subtle level, it is the conflict between two quite different attitudes. Sammy is easy going and romantic in the sense of having a high regard for people and a low opinion of rigid rules and regulations. He also has a low regard for the commercial products which are sold in supermarkets. The manager, on the other hand, appears to take the store very seriously and is a stickler for the rules. In terms of outlook, these two characters are at opposite ends of a spectrum. The conflict between them is not only the mainspring of the plot, it dramatizes the theme as well.

Another type of dramatic conflict pits a protagonist against a group or society as a whole. Langston Hughes' "On the Road" is a good example. The protagonist, Sargeant, is an unemployed black man who has been rebuffed by "hundreds of relief shelters during the depression years." The rejection by the minister suggests a larger rejection by society as a whole. Sargeant's rebellion is not against an individual but against all of authority—the church and all those in control. At the end of the story, when his apparent success is revealed as only a dream, the police are seen as representing that same brutal and insensitive society.

A similar sort of conflict is seen when a character struggles with some aspect of nature. Most accounts of mountain climbing describe the protagonist as "battling" the elements and the mountain itself. Novels like Conrad's *Typhoon* and Hemingway's *The Old Man and the Sea* place an individual in conflict with the sea. What makes them more than mere adventure stories is the degree to which each work explores the subtleties of theme and character. The conflict has not been muted, but other elements have been added.

Finally, dramatic conflict often takes the form of an inner struggle. It is natural for us to think of a person as being "of two minds" or "debating with oneself." Although it is a metaphor, the notion of a divided self is a familiar one to all of us.

There is little of this in a story like "On the Road" in which the conflict is essentially external—between a man and society; but in Carson Mc-Cullers' "The Sojourner," the conflict is almost entirely internal. The protagonist, John Ferris, feels no antagonism toward his former wife or her husband and they, in turn, are most cordial to him. The struggle in that story is within Ferris himself. The portion of him which has enjoyed an independent life without responsibilities is opposed by his new longing for warm, enduring relationships.

When we analyze dramatic conflict in a story or novel we tend to focus on one particular type. But keep in mind that even in a relatively short work of fiction there may be several different forms of conflict—sometimes occurring simultaneously in the same scene. This is the case in "Small Point Bridge."

As the story opens, the emphasis is on Isaac Bates' struggle with nature. It is an achievement to have survived "still another Maine winter." His relationship with the harsh elements takes the form of a personal antagonism. Not until well into the story does the conflict shift to man-against-man. He and his old associate, Seth, have become *antagonists*. At the height of their struggle there on the bridge, Isaac also contends with an inner debate. We are not given his thoughts directly, but his uncertainty is clear from his actions. His decision to return to Seth's house resolves the conflict between the two of them, and at the end of the story they are unified in their shared efforts against the forces of nature. The dramatic impact of the story depends not on any one type of conflict but on a closely connected series.

DRAMATIC QUESTIONS

Simple fiction establishes curiosity right from the start with what commercial writers call *the hook*. The first paragraph is blatantly designed to hold the reader—gun shots, a speeding car, and the like. The technique is familiar to anyone who watches television.

Writers of sophisticated fiction employ a similar but more subtle technique called *dramatic questions*. They are not limited to openings. They are questions which hold our attention and keep us reading. What will happen, we wonder at the beginning of "The Sojourner," when this man visits his former wife and her new husband? Later we wonder whether he will change his ways when he returns to Paris. What's going to happen, we ask in "On the Road," when Sargeant knocks at the door of a parsonage on a snowy night? As soon as that question is answered, we are astonished by his ability to knock the whole church down, "covering the cops and the people with bricks and stones and debris." What's going on? When we finally learn the harsh reality, the story is over.

Dramatic questions are generated from each individual work and so are highly varied, but there are some basic types which recur fairly regularly: *Will he or she succeed? Will she or he discover what we already know? Will a compromise be found? Will this episode end in violence? Why is he or she behaving in this apparently unmotivated way? Who did it?*

In relatively simple works, the major dramatic question is frequently the theme itself. Murder mysteries are described as "whodunits" and often that question is as much theme as the novel contains. Stories of pure adventure may have no more theme than the simple question of survival. But in literary works, dramatic questions tend to be a means to an end. They generate interest and help to dramatize and highlight themes which are more complex. When Sargeant appears to knock the church down, for example, the author has created a highly effective dramatic question, but the theme of that story involves social issues (the poor versus those in power), moral concerns, race relations, and the role of the church.

Dramatic questions are a type of tension in that your desire to find out is pitted against the author's refusal to reveal what you want to know at that point. If you look at it this way you will realize how important *withheld information* is in almost every work of fiction. To understand how a story or novel manages to hold your attention, look closely at what is *not* being revealed at a particular point.

Often you cannot analyze the technique until after you have finished a particular scene and are able to look back. For example, not until you are more than halfway into "Small Point Bridge" can you see what Isaac Bates' real motive is in visiting Seth on that particular day. Only after finishing "On the Road" can you see how Langston Hughes has created a strong sense of curiosity in most readers by not revealing that the scene of apparent victory is in fact a dream.

When you review the pattern of dramatic questions in a work of fiction you may notice that they form a rhythm of increasing tension followed by a release. These are sometimes referred to as *rising action* and the release as a *resolution*. These terms, originally applied to drama, are helpful in explaining the dynamic quality of fiction.

Suspense

Suspense is created when a dramatic question is expanded and intensified. We say a work is "suspenseful" when we have the feeling that we are moving from one dramatic question to another without a break. One might think that this would be the most effective form of fiction and that all authors would try to achieve it. But there is a trade-off here just as there is with almost every literary technique. Suspense holds attention, but if it is pushed too far it tends to dominate or even obliterate subtler elements such as characterization and complexity of theme. Novels which are advertised as "highly suspenseful" are sometimes the sort which are quickly read and just as quickly forgotten.

Surprise

Surprise creates dramatic impact through an unexpected twist of the plot, new information, or an abrupt shift in the attitude of a character. In a sense it is the opposite of suspense since instead of withholding information it suddenly provides it—often when you least expect it.

One of the most dramatic examples in the stories you have read is the final scene in "On the Road." "'This ain't no train,'" Sargeant is told, "'You in jail.'" The tone of the story suddenly changes. We had begun to accept the work as a lighthearted fantasy in which the protagonist meets and talks with a sympathetic and understanding figure of Christ. But suddenly we realize that this story is not a fantasy. It is a harshly realistic and bitter work.

More frequently, surprise stems from some abrupt shift in a character's attitude. This occurs in "Small Point Bridge" when we realize that what seemed to be a pleasant social call is in fact a visit with a serious intent. An old friendship suddenly erupts into a bitter antagonism. Consider how much impact would have been lost if the story had started off by giving all the facts: "This was the day Isaac Bates would have to collect token rent from Seth—either that or see Seth take possession over the land he had been using." True, that version would provide a dramatic question of sorts, but the surprise element midway in the story would be lost.

Surprises like these have to catch the reader unawares to be effective, but for the sake of credibility they also have to be logically integrated with the plot and consistent with character. If you review the work when you are finished, you can usually see how the author prepared for such shifts.

In "A & P," for example, Sammy's dramatic rebellion against the store and its rigid dress code has been prepared for by his highly critical attitude toward the products sold there. When we review the story, we can see that he had a strong sense of values from the start.

In "On the Road," the preparation for that final jolt is established by hints in the plot itself. If you look carefully you will find the exact point where the story shifts from Sargeant's waking experience to what we later realize is a dream. The scene is the one in which Sargeant is struggling to get into the church and the police begin to beat him. The key sentence is, "And then the church fell down." This is in itself a surprise and we assume that the story has become some kind of fantasy. It is also a preparation for the concluding surprise when we discover that what we took to be fantasy is only a dream and we, like Sargeant, are jolted back into harsh reality.

In "Small Point Bridge," I made a conscious effort to prepare for

Isaac's apparent shift in character. As the dispute between the two men grows more intense, Isaac switches from his friendly self to harsh self-interest. This might seem like a violation of his character if there were not numerous indications earlier that he is an almost brutally stubborn man when it comes to dealing with nature. It shouldn't seem illogical that he, if pressed, would apply the same toughness to his old friend and associate.

When the sense of surprise in fiction is intensified, it becomes *shock*. Used sparingly, this can be an effective device. The police brutality at the end of "On the Road" is a good example. But when shock is repeated frequently in a novel or a story, we sometimes have the feeling that it is being used as an end in itself. That is when *dramatic* fiction becomes *melodramatic*.

The distinction between *drama* and *melodrama* in fiction is not precise. But we can all agree on the extreme cases, and the terms are certainly valuable. Fiction is called *dramatic* when the various forms of tension discussed in this chapter are used effectively but unobtrusively—that is, when the plot is charged with conflict, dramatic questions, suspense, surprise, and perhaps an occasional moment of shock. But when those elements are allowed to dominate a work, are poorly prepared for, and are stressed at the expense of subtle characterization or thematic elements, then we feel that our emotions are being manipulated. That is when we can say that the work has become *melodramatic*.

If, for example, "Small Point Bridge" dealt with a foreign agent with a code name of "Seth" who struggles to conceal a "shack" which is in fact a secret control center for an unnamed foreign power, and in the final scene our hero, Isaac Bates, throws his antagonist between grinding slabs of ice, we would have high melodrama.

Fictional works which deal with war, spies, terrorism, horror, and the supernatural are often (but not always) intentionally melodramatic—as are their film counterparts. Such works can be highly entertaining, but they tend to be fairly simple in theme and characterization.

EXAMINING TENSION

With short works, you will probably want to postpone your analysis of the narrative tensions until you have finished your first reading. There is much to be said for allowing yourself a direct experience of the work without being too analytical the first time through.

But while the material is still fresh in your mind, take a few minutes to examine how the various types of tension have been used to hold your interest and keep the work dynamic. Since dramatic conflict is often the most apparent, start with that. Was it person-against-person or was a character pitted against a group or force of nature? To what degree has an inner struggle been a part of this work? Be prepared for plenty of variation. As we saw in "On the Road," the tension in some stories is almost entirely external. On the other hand, in stories like "The Sojourner," conflict can be essentially internal. Usually there is a combination.

Then identify the various dramatic questions which helped to hold your interest in your first reading. In highly dramatic works, you may find that just as soon as one is answered, another is raised. In gentler stories and novels, the questions may be more diffuse and may deal more with character than with plot.

Finally, examine those moments in the story when you felt surprise. They may be as mild as not expecting an easy-going supermarket clerk to quit his job because of three young women he has never met. In more dramatic stories, they can be as powerful as a character pulling down a church. Whether the moment of surprise is slight or a real jolt, examine carefully how the author has prepared for it.

With novels, don't wait to finish the entire work before examining how tension is being employed. Stop every few chapters and ask these same questions. Take some notes. Often you will find that a few minutes of periodic analysis as you move through a novel will help you to draw much more from the work as a whole.

TOPICS FOR ANALYSIS

The following questions, like those which conclude earlier chapters, can be used to stimulate your own thought, to initiate class discussion, or to serve as topics for short papers.

1. Read "On the Road" once more for a close analysis. Pick out (a) each sample of conflict between individuals or groups, (b) each sentence which establishes a new dramatic question, and (c) each sentence which gave you a jolt of surprise. This exercise requires closer reading than you normally give a work of fiction, but it will provide an insight into how tension in fiction is established.

2. Select a short story (or an extended scene from a novel) *not* included in this volume which provides an example of conflict. Describe the type of conflict (person against person? inner struggle? against nature?) and the degree (subtle? dramatic?). Now describe what would be left if this conflict were removed. (Don't say "nothing"; something always remains.)

3. Select another fictional conflict not discussed in this volume and analyze it in the same way. Then heighten the conflict as it might be in a spy novel, a war story, or some melodramatic television drama. Describe what it would be like or actually write a satiric version. Enjoy yourself. Conclude with a brief analysis of what makes your version melodramatic.

4. Review a short story or a lengthy scene from a novel and identify two or three dramatic questions which help to hold your interest. Locate the sentence or sentences which withhold information from the reader. Then rewrite those sen-

tences so that they answer the questions prematurely. (Example from "On the Road": "He thought he was pulling the church down, but actually he was dreaming.") Describe what the story or scene would be like with your revisions.

5.   Analyze a surprising turn of events in a story or a novel you have read. How did it reverse or at least revise your expectations? Now examine the ways in which the author prepared for the event (often aspects of character or apparently casual references or lines of dialogue). If you find none, is the turn of events explained in some logical way later?

Tension generates the energy contained in a story or novel. It is what keeps it moving. If you look closely at the lines of tension in a work of fiction, you will see what gives it life.

chapter 10

EXCERPTS FROM TWO NOVELS

from **Maud Martha** *by Gwendolyn Brooks, published by Harper & Row, Publishers, Inc.*

What had been wanted was this always, this always to last, the talking softly on this porch, with the snake plant in the jardiniere in the southwest corner, and the obstinate slip from Aunt Eppie's magnificent Michigan fern at the left side of the friendly door. Mama, Maud Martha and Helen rocked slowly in their rocking chairs, and looked at the late afternoon light on the lawn, and at the emphatic iron of the fence and at the poplar tree. These things might soon be theirs no longer. Those shafts and pools of light, the tree, the graceful iron, might soon be viewed possessively by different eyes.

Papa was to have gone that noon, during his lunch hour, to the office of the Home Owners' Loan. If he had not succeeded in getting another extension, they would be leaving this house in which they had lived for more than fourteen years. There was little hope. The Home Owners' Loan was hard. They sat, making their plans.

"We'll be moving into a nice flat somewhere," said Mama. "Somewhere on South Park, or Michigan, or in Washington Park Court." Those flats, as the girls and Mama knew well, were burdens on wages twice the size of Papa's. This was not mentioned now.

"They're much prettier than this old house," said Helen. "I have friends I'd just as soon not bring here. And I have other friends that wouldn't come down this far for anything, unless they were in a taxi."

Yesterday, Maud Martha would have attacked her. Tomorrow she might. Today she said nothing. She merely gazed at a little hopping robin in the tree, her tree, and tried to keep the fronts of her eyes dry.

"Well, I do know," said Mama, turning her hands over and over, "that I've been getting tireder and tireder of doing that firing. From October to April, there's firing to be done."

"But lately we've been helping, Harry and I," said Maud Martha. "And sometimes in March and April and in October, and even in November, we could build a little fire in the fireplace. Sometimes the weather was just right for that."

She knew, from the way they looked at her, that this had been a mistake. They did not want to cry.

But she felt that the little line of white, somewhat ridged with smoked purple, and all that cream-shot saffron, would never drift across any western sky except that in back of this house. The rain would drum with as sweet a dullness nowhere but here. The birds on South Park were mechanical birds, no better than the poor caught canaries in those "rich" women's sun parlors.

"It's just going to kill Papa!" burst out Maud Martha. "He loves this house! He *lives* for this house!"

"He lives for us," said Helen. "It's us he loves. He wouldn't want the house, except for us."

"And he'll have us," added Mama, "wherever."

"You know," Helen sighed, "if you want to know the truth, this is a relief. If this hadn't come up, we would have gone on, just dragged on, hanging out here forever."

"It might," allowed Mama, "be an act of God. God may just have reached down, and picked up the reins."

"Yes," Maud Martha cracked in, "that's what you always say— that God knows best."

Her mother looked at her quickly, decided the statement was not suspect, looked away.

Helen saw Papa coming. "There's Papa," said Helen.

They could not tell a thing from the way Papa was walking. It was that same dear little staccato walk, one shoulder down, then the other, then repeat, and repeat. They watched his progress. He passed the Kennedys', he passed the vacant lot, he passed Mrs. Blakemore's. They wanted to hurl themselves over the fence, into the street, and shake the truth out of his collar. He opened his gate—the gate—and still his stride and face told them nothing.

"Hello," he said.

Mama got up and followed him through the front door. The girls knew better than to go in too.

Presently Mama's head emerged. Her eyes were lamps turned on.

"It's all right," she exclaimed. "He got it. It's all over. Everything is all right."

The door slammed shut. Mama's footsteps hurried away.

"I think," said Helen, rocking rapidly, "I think I'll give a party. I haven't given a party since I was eleven. I'd like some of my friends to just casually see that we're homeowners."

from **A Mother and Two Daughters**
by Gail Godwin, published by
The Viking Press, 1982

Nell closed the book and sighed.

She recalled a hot August day in 1942. One of those true "dog days" when you sat very still and imagined Heaven as a cool body of water in which you could drench yourself. She was six months pregnant with Lydia, and, in those days, visibly pregnant women did not parade themselves at swimming pools. But Leonard's father, who had a car, was coming to take them out to a lake.

Well, he came. But they never got to the lake. Cate, who was three at the time, bounded out to the car with her bucket and shovel. Her grandfather, smoking one of his strong cigars, reached across and opened the passenger's door. "Come on, missy. Ride up front with the old man."

But Cate had taken one whiff of the inside of the car and said, "*Pe*-yew! I'm not riding in that smelly car."

"How are you going to get to the lake, then?"

By the time Nell and Leonard reached the car, Strickland Senior was visibly angry, but there was still a chance of reconciliation.

"She says she won't ride in this 'smelly car,'" Leonard's father reported to his son. "Can't you all bring up your little gal better than that?"

"Cate," said Leonard, "apologize at once to Grandpop. Say 'I'm sorry, Grandpop.'"

"No," said three-year-old Cate.

"You don't apologize, I'm going to drive off without you," said old Strickland menacingly. "Your momma and daddy and I will just drive off and leave you here all by yourself."

"I don't care," said the child. But she looked frightened.

Nell took Cate back toward the house and tried to reason with her in a low voice. "Honey, you've hurt Grandpop's feelings. Nobody likes to be told their car is smelly. Just say you're sorry, like a good girl, and climb in the car and try not to think about the smell, and soon we'll be at a nice cool lake. Won't that be nice?"

"No. He's mean. And the car *smells!*"

"Cate, please. It's so hot and we'd all like to go to the lake."

"Go on, then," said the child, and marched up to the front door and stood with her straight little back to them, holding her pail and shovel. No threats or entreaties could budge that rigid little figure.

Leonard suggested that he stay behind so that Nell, who was heavy and uncomfortable, could go to the lake with his father.

Nell, by this time in tears, insisted Leonard go alone with his father, and she would stay home and discipline Cate.

"Well, dammit, you all two make up your minds," old Strickland had shouted at last, curling up his lip to show his teeth, browned from cigars. He was mad and hurt; he had taken a fancy to Cate—or as near a fancy as a selfish man like himself could take.

The result was, Mr. Strickland had driven away all by himself, Leonard had taken Cate back in the house and pulled down the pants of her little swimsuit and smacked her bottom, she screaming all the while in an unrepentant little chant, "It *smells,* it *smells!*" And the family had spent the remainder of the day prostrate with heat and out of sorts with one another. "What a will that child has," Leonard had remarked after Cate was asleep, and Nell had been furious and disdainful of the admiration in his tone.

Yes, it smelled, thought Nell, thirty-seven summers later. A lot of things smell. But people are more important.

chapter 11

STRUCTURE: SCENES AND PLOT

SELECTIVITY

Fiction is never the whole story. If an author tried to record all the events that occurred in a given period of time, the result would not only be lengthy, it would also be stupifyingly dull. As a result, fiction is always selective.

In this respect, fiction is similar to our own memories. If someone were to ask you what you did yesterday, you would find that you had already forgotten a number of routine activities. Not only that, you would probably *choose* to ignore whatever seemed unimportant. Who wants to hear whether you brushed your teeth or what you had for breakfast?

In your account of what you did yesterday you would also probably group your activities into manageable units: "Right after breakfast I went to the Post Office . . . ." "In the early afternoon I worked on a term paper and . . . ." "But at 3:00 I went over to the gym."

Writers of fiction usually divide their narratives in much the same way—except that the decisions of what to include and what to leave out are made more consciously and with more factors in mind. The units of action they use are fictional *scenes,* and the arrangement of those scenes is called *plot.*

THE FICTIONAL SCENE

A scene in fiction is a unit of action usually identified by place (the setting), a particular character or group of characters, and occasionally by activity. Some scenes are clearly designated. Others are so hazy it is difficult to see just where they begin and end. Good fiction doesn't have to be rigidly divided into scenes, but the concept is a helpful one if you are going to look closely at the way a story or novel is constructed.

Most short stories are made up of several scenes, but it is possible to write a sophisticated story which is limited to just one. John Updike's story "A & P" comes close to this pattern.

The story begins with the three girls walking into the supermarket in their bathing suits. The action proceeds in a regular sequence to their departure and Sammy's grand gesture of quitting. The entire story to this point is one sustained scene. Only in the very last paragraph does the setting shift: ". . . the door heaves itself open, and outside the sunshine is skating around on the asphalt." Here Sammy is alone (shift in the characters present) and the setting is distinctly different. He looks back through the windows, and sees the manager taking over the abandoned register.

"A & P" is almost a one-scene story. It is not simple in terms of character revelation or thematic suggestion, but with the exception of that last paragraph it is a single narrative unit.

Novels can contain scenes which are just as unified—though almost always there are many of them. The selection from the novel *Maud Martha* by Gwendolyn Brooks is an example. It is written like a sketch or very brief short story. Neither characterization nor theme are developed as fully as they would in a story intended to stand on its own, but all the elements are there: A dramatic situation is established, a group of characters deal with it, and there is a resolution at the end. We can call this a *dramatic scene* because it has the kind of emotional impact and unity of action we associate with plays.

Sometimes a scene deals with a single character who is alone. The opening scenes of "The Sojourner" and "Small Point Bridge" are similar in that the protagonist of each story is introduced in isolation—John Ferris, you remember, is waking up in a New York hotel room, and Isaac Bates is standing by his living-room window looking out over his property on a raw day in March. More often, scenes involve characters in interaction—like Sargeant in "On the Road" dealing with the insensitive minister on a snowy night.

The scene, then, is an important unit of fiction which occasionally stands alone as the basis of a relatively brief short story but which more often is a basic unit in the construction of a story or novel. It is to fiction what the cell is to biological structures.

CHRONOLOGICAL PLOTS

Plot is often described as the sequence of events in fiction. This is accurate, but it is more helpful to think of plot as the arrangement of scenes. When the fictional scenes are arranged in the order in which they occurred, we call this a *chronological plot.*

The simplest sort of chronological plot merely places one scene after another like pearls on a string. This is not a common approach, but *Maud Martha,* the novel from which the excerpt in the previous chapter was taken, is a fine example. Each chapter is a separate scene. Although these scenes all deal with one character and are arranged in chronological order over a period of years, they are essentially independent episodes. The connections between them, and indeed the unity of the work as a whole, is based not on plot in the usual sense but on character. Reading these scenes is like looking at photos in an album; through them we come to know Maud Martha as a person.

If this approach interests you, read the whole novel. It is brief and sensitively done. In addition, consider two novels by Evan S. Connell, Jr.: *Mr. Bridge* and *Mrs. Bridge.* They also create vivid character studies through a sequence of chronological but essentially unconnected scenes.

It is much more common, however, for plot in both novels and short stories to be built on causation—that is, because this happens, that happens; and as a result of that, new events occur. Each scene in some way shapes the next.

"Small Point Bridge" has a chronological plot in which the scenes are linked in this way. The story opens with Isaac standing at his living-room window, reflecting on his continuing battle with the elements. The view reminds him that it is the last day of March, and he sets out in his Jeep—the second scene. The third scene is in Seth's simple cabin. Although we don't know then why Isaac is there, we do know that it has something to do with the date. This was established in the first scene.

At the end of their conversation, we learn that Isaac is insisting on token rent to maintain ownership of the land. The discussion turns to argument, and because of this Isaac leaves the cabin and steps out onto the footbridge. Because he goes out at that particular moment, he sees the damage the ice is doing to the cannery, and because of that Seth is lured out. Because they are caught there faced with the larger threat of the winter ice, Isaac changes his mind and goes back in with Seth. And because he has done that, he has allowed Seth to take legal possession of the property. Notice how this description is essentially "because of this, that happens." The scenes are interlocked with causation, each creating the circumstances of the next.

This same pattern is usually found in novels. Since the units are often longer, it is important to keep the scenes straight in your mind or in your notes. Remember that in all but the simplest fiction, *what* happens is no more important than *why* it happens.

MULTITRACK PLOTS

In a multitrack novel two or more plots are developed in a parallel way. There is almost always some kind of linkage between the primary story and the *subplot,* but each has its own structure.

One of the more famous examples of this is *Anna Karenina* by Leo Tolstoi. The main story deals with Anna, whose marriage begins to crumble at the beginning of the novel. Her adulterous love affair erodes her life, bringing her in stages toward eventual suicide. In an extended subplot, the novel also deals with a character named Levin who becomes almost as important as the protagonist. As Anna's problems become more hopelessly complex, Levin and his young wife slowly build a simple and loving life together. A brief description like this makes the plot appear contrived, but in the novel itself these characters become a convincing and subtle contrast, one in a tragic decline and the other moving toward fulfillment.

A more recent example is *A Mother and Two Daughters* by Gail Godwin, a portion of which you just read in the previous chapter. In this novel there are actually three "tracks" since the emphasis is almost equally distributed among these three women. Although they are together some of the time, the novel explores their lives separately as well, shifting the point of view from one to the next.

This concept of multiple plots can be pushed further until the work becomes a kind of mosaic. John Dos Passos' *U.S.A.,* for example, is a trilogy which gives a panoramic picture of life in this country from World War I to the beginning of the Depression in the early 1930s. The author moves from character to character, frequently returning to continue the narrative of those previously introduced. The effect is like reading a number of different short stories at the same time, shifting back and forth from one to the other. Another example of this same technique is Norman Mailer's novel about World War II, *The Naked and the Dead.* Novels like these create a broad picture, often historical. Although characterization sometimes suffers with such a technique, the advantage is being able to present a sweeping view of history. Both of these works, for example, are highly readable and entertaining as well as being important social documents.

EPISODIC PLOTS

Although some multitrack novels are made up of short episodes, the term *episodic novel* has a special meaning. It refers to novels which are unified by a single protagonist who goes through one adventure after another. Action is commonly the dominant mode, but the series of adventures often do not lead to a grand climax. Generally they do not have much effect on the protagonist either. He or she is essentially the same at the end of the work as at the beginning. One way to judge whether a novel is truly episodic is to ask yourself whether you could change the order of most chapters and not be confused.

This may seem at first to be a rather unstructured way to write fiction, but it is the pattern in such works as Cervantes' *Don Quixote* and Gabriel Garcia Marquez' *One Hundred Years of Solitude.*

The term *picaresque* refers to a particular type of episodic novel in which the protagonist, usually telling his or her own story in the first person, is a rogue or, in contemporary terms, a street-wise and often comic survivor. Don Quixote is really too naive to be classified as a picaresque hero, but the incredible Moll Flanders in Daniel Defoe's novel of the same name is a perfect example. Born in prison, married five times (once to her own brother), serving twelve years as a prostitute, twelve years as a thief, eight years in prison, she ends up rich and penitent! Though written in 1722, this novel is still highly entertaining.

A more recent example of a picaresque novel is *The Ginger Man* by J. P. Donleavy. Set in contemporary Ireland, this work deals with a self-centered, hard-drinking, sentimental, utterly dishonest male chauvinist American who manages to live off a series of women. Like *Moll Flanders,* this novel is comic, realistic, and loosely plotted. The central character never really develops. The work is plot-dominated.

There is another similarity between these two works which is complex and worth close examination: Like almost all picaresque novels, they are written as satires. The protagonists are held up to ridicule. But it is an open question as to whether we read such works mainly to cast scorn on these outrageous characters or whether we secretly admire their behavior. This is a subject well worth considering whenever reading or writing about a picaresque novel.

NONCHRONOLOGICAL PLOTS

In a nonchronological plot, the scenes are presented in a different order from that in which they occurred. This may seem at first to be a purely literary technique, but actually it is one we all use quite naturally in daily conversation. We say, "I had a terrible argument with her which has really complicated everything, but first let me tell you how it started." Or, "The trip started off badly when Harry refused to take the plane. Everyone thought he was just being ridiculous, and I did too at the time. But listen to what he went through the last time he flew. . . ." In both cases the speaker began with a dramatic moment and then went back to fill in earlier incidents. It does not seem at all strange to shift the order of our narration even in conversation.

Since nonchronological plots can get fairly complicated, it helps if we distinguish the *factual sequence* from the *narrative sequence*. The first is the order in which the events occurred. The latter is the order in which the author has presented them.

Each of the two brief conversational examples just given would, if used in fiction, be an introduction to a *flashback*. This is a literary term which came from film writing. A flashback is not just a reference to a past event; it is an entire scene which moves us as readers back to a previous event. If we developed the conversational fragment into a literary flashback, it might come out like this:

> I had a terrible argument with her which really complicated things, but first let me tell you how it started. I had been up all night preparing a report which was overdue and was still not finished. I drank so much coffee my hands were shaking. It was nine the next morning when I saw her and she started giving me a hard time about going around unshaved.

Flashbacks can be much longer, of course, and they can be introduced more subtly than with phrases like "but first let me tell you . . . ." One technique which they almost always share, however, is the use of the past perfect tense. Although many readers don't have the slightest idea what the past perfect tense is, they know that, "I *had* been up all night . . ." means that the events which follow took place at an earlier time.

One never has trouble with simple flashbacks. But occasionally if you are reading fast you will miss the initial clue which introduces a longer flashback. This can be very confusing. In such cases, try to locate where the flashback began by finding the sentence—often the beginning of a paragraph—which uses the past perfect, "had." In the same way, the end of the flashback may be identified by a second use of the past perfect: "That had been one of the best vacations ever," or "She had never mentioned it to anyone." Or it may be clear enough from the context and phrased in the simple past: "That was all years ago."

Many stories—particularly short ones—do not contain any flashbacks. The technique is helpful but also disruptive. It lends itself to longer works. The selection from Gail Godwin's novel *A Mother and Two Daughters* is itself a complete flashback. The author does not use the past perfect to introduce it, but instead makes the shift in time through phrasing: "She recalled a hot August day in 1942." Clear enough. But notice that she does use the past perfect to end the flashback:

> The result was, Mr. Strickland had driven away all by himself, Leonard had taken Cate back in the house and pulled down the pants of her little swimsuit and smacked her bottom . . . . And the family had spent the remainder of the day prostrate with heat and out of sorts with one another.

Most authors use flashbacks sparingly, but occasionally you will find a work in which multiple flashbacks are used so frequently that they have become the primary organizational device. In these cases, the narrative sequence has almost nothing to do with the actual sequence. Such stories and novels are often (but not always) written in the first person. The narrator recalls first one aspect of an experience and then another. The unity is achieved not by the linkage of one scene to the next in the order of their occurrence but by the association of ideas in the narrator's mind. William Faulkner's story "A Rose for Emily" does this without a clearly defined narrator. We hear fragments of the story the way we might pick up information from listening to townspeople talking about a local scandal. Joseph Conrad's *Lord Jim* is a good example of the technique used in a novel.

Another form of the nonchronological plot is the *frame story*. Such works often begin with a narrator who then either tells a story or introduces another character who has a tale to tell. In a sense, the body of the story has become one long flashback. Often the initial scene includes other characters who serve as listeners, though that is not absolutely necessary. At the end of a frame story the narrator usually appears again, commenting on the story just told. The "frame" is the narrator.

About the best-known example of a frame story is Chaucer's *The Canterbury Tales*. A group of pilgrims from a wide variety of backgrounds gather at an inn, and each tells a story. There are frequent interruptions and commentaries to remind the reader of the immediate surroundings.

Chaucer, writing at the end of the fourteenth century, was using a form which was already popular both with narrative verse and prose. *The Decameron*, a collection of tales written by Giovanni Boccaccio a century earlier, used a similar approach—though Chaucer may never have read it. The many stories collected under the general title of *A Thousand and One Nights* are unified in somewhat the same manner.

More recent examples of the frame story usually have a single narrator who tells just one story. Joseph Conrad used this approach frequently. In his novella, *Youth*, for example, an unnamed narrator recalls hearing a man named Marlow tell a long story about his first adventure at sea. In this way, *Youth* is a frame within a frame. Unlike *The Canterbury Tales*, this story consists of one lengthy tale told by a single narrator. We would almost forget that it was being told to friends on board an anchored ship if Marlow did not from time to time interrupt his own story with the phrase, "Pass the bottle." The frame is completed at the end when the original observer describes Marlow and his group of friends sitting around the table.

Why go to all that trouble? There are different kinds of advantages to different types of frame stories. In some cases it is merely a way of unifying a group of stories which would otherwise seem scattered. In Conrad's *Youth* it allows the author to present two "voices," the naive and enthusiastic tone of Marlow as a young man and the calmer, more detached view of the older man looking back. Having a narrator recall Marlow telling the story gives the author a way to describe both the narrator and his listeners. The technique seems complicated when described, but it is not at all difficult to follow in the reading.

The *front-framed story* is simply a variation of this. It begins like a conventional frame story, but there is no return to the narrator at the end. What remains of the frame is merely an introduction. Although the term is not in general use, the reverse of a front-framed story could be called "back framed." Philip Roth's *Portnoy's Complaint* is a good example. At the end of the last chapter in this first-person novel the voice of a doctor is heard. We realize only then that the entire novel is to be seen as a monologue delivered by a patient to an extraordinarily silent psychiatrist.

TIME DISTORTION

When a work of fiction distorts time, the result is not necessarily non-chronological. The plot may move forward but at a pace which is erratic.

Langston Hughes' story "On the Road" contains a good example of that. The opening scene is realistic and moves at a conventional pace. But the scene in which Sargeant talks with Christ is a dream and may have occurred in an instant. At the end of the story we realize that he has ended up in a jail. Time has swept by—confusing us for a moment just as it did Sargeant.

Another famous example of this technique is the often-anthologized story "An Occurrence at Owl Creek Bridge" by Ambrose Bierce. In that story a man during the Civil War is about to be hanged from a bridge. The rope breaks, however, and he plunges into the river, escaping with great difficulty and eventually making it back to his home and his wife—or so we think. In the last sentence we learn that this has all been a fantasy in that split second between the time the board fell away beneath his feet and his death.

These are dramatic examples. In novels the technique can be used in more subtle and elaborate ways. If time distortion interests you, try reading a novel called *Briefing for a Descent into Hell* by Doris Lessing. It is a complex work and requires careful reading, but it develops the distortion of time in fascinating ways.

REVIEWING THE STRUCTURE

When you are in the middle of a story or a novel, you are probably too close to the material to see the structure of the plot clearly. You should make a point of identifying particular scenes, especially those which are the bases of flashbacks. But the time for a full review of the narrative structure is immediately after you have finished the work.

Your analysis of short stories will be on an entirely different scale than that of novels. It is easy to find and review those scenes which seem particularly important. When you finish a story like John Updike's "A & P," for example, take a second look at that shift in scene at the end. It is significant that a character who has objected to what he takes to be an insulting enforcement of the rules now is outside and, looking back, sees that his place has been taken by the one for whom the rules are very important. This is a small detail, but that little shift in scene sharpens and clarifies the theme of the story.

The crucial scene in Langston Hughes' story "On the Road" is the one which we discover at the end is really the protagonist's dream. Exactly where did it start, and where did it end? How would the tone of the story change if the author had ended the story with Sargeant saying "so long" to Christ? I will return to tone in Chapter 13, but it is worth noticing here how the deletion of the final scene in a story like this can turn a harshly realistic tone into one which might be described as wistful longing.

In a story like "Small Point Bridge," notice how in some scenes Isaac Bates seems to be dealing directly with the forces of nature, and in others he turns his energy against his old friend, Seth. That should help you to see that the protagonist in this story really has two antagonists: nature and his old friend. In the final scene there is only one enemy, the force of nature. If you look at each scene in terms of conflict, you will see how the structure of the story contributes to the theme.

When dealing with novels, your examination cannot be as detailed. But it will be even more important to see the overall structure of the plot. It may help you to analyze the pattern in terms of rising and falling action—an approach first proposed by Aristotle in examining the structure of Greek drama. Many loosely structured novels simply don't lend themselves to this type of analysis, but others can almost be diagramed in those terms. The protagonist may start off in a good position in terms of health, power, or security and then begin a long downward path. Or a conflict between two characters may be used as the central organizing force, and the resolution serve as the culmination of the novel. Another pattern is to have the protagonist descend from good fortune to bad while a second character climbs steadily to a position of strength and security. As we have seen, this is the pattern in Tolstoi's *Anna Karenina*. It also applies to *Tender is the Night* by F. Scott Fitzgerald, a novel which is in other respects quite different.

In the case of *A Mother and Two Daughters* from which the selection was taken in the previous chapter, the initial crisis is the death of the father in the family. The structure of the novel is based essentially on the various ways the widow and her two adult daughters cope with this new situation. You can't diagram the rising and falling action the way you can for some works, but you can see an overall pattern if you review the structure as soon as you have finished the last chapter. Each of the three characters moves from a state of severe personal dislocation to a different type of rebirth.

TOPICS FOR ANALYSIS

If you are writing a paper on structure and have a relatively free choice of subject, here are some directions you might consider:

1.   Analyze the structure of a short story which contains several scenes. How are the scenes linked by cause and effect? How do they build toward the high point or *climax* of the work?

2.   Select two well-defined scenes from a novel. In what ways does each resemble a short story? On the other hand, what keeps them from standing alone? (Consider not only mechanical details like the need to fill in factual information, but thematic concerns as well.)

3.   If you have recently read a multitrack novel, analyze what would be lost if the work were published with only the major plot. (Film versions of novels often do this). Try to be as specific as possible.

4.   Select a fictional work (story or novel) which is not a frame story. Then suggest a frame. That is, describe a narrator who presents the material—either in the third person or the first—at the beginning and then concludes it at the end. Try to defend your version by showing what you have added to the work. (If that strikes you as presumptuous, you might conclude your paper with an explanation of why the author probably wouldn't agree with your proposed revisions.)

All this is designed to help you look closely at the structure of what you read. It is possible, of course, to enjoy a story or a novel without this kind of close analysis. In the case of simple fiction, this is probably the best approach. But with sophisticated fiction—long or short—you will draw far more satisfaction if you take the time to examine the structure. It will not only reveal the construction of the work, but it will also help you to see other aspects such as tone, theme, and character development. The plot alone—what happens—is the surface; when you examine the structure, the deliberate arrangement of scenes, you are seeing the story in depth.

chapter 12

EXCERPTS FROM TWO NOVELS

from **Youth** *by Joseph Conrad,**
originally published in 1902 and
available in a number of
paperback editions

"Then we entered the Indian Ocean and steered northerly for Java Head. The winds were light. Weeks slipped by. She crawled on, do or die, and people at home began to think of posting us as overdue.

"One Saturday evening, I being off duty, the men asked me to give them an extra bucket of water or so—for washing clothes. As I did not wish to screw on the fresh-water pump so late, I went forward whistling, and with a key in my hand to unlock the forepeak scuttle, intending to serve the water out of a spare tank we kept there.

"The smell down below was as unexpected as it was frightful. One would have thought hundreds of paraffin-lamps had been flaring and smoking in that hole for days. I was glad to get out. The man with me coughed and said, 'Funny smell, sir.' I answered negligently, 'It's good for the health they say,' and walked aft.

"The first thing I did was to put my head down the square of the midship ventilator. As I lifted the lid a visible breath, something like a thin fog, a puff of faint haze, rose from the opening. The ascending air was hot, and had a heavy, sooty, paraffiny smell. I gave one sniff, and put down the lid gently. It was no use choking myself. The cargo was on fire.

"Next day she began to smoke in earnest. You see it was to be expected, for though the coal was of a safe kind, that cargo had been so handled, so broken up with handling, that it looked more like smithy coal than anything else. Then it had been wetted—more than once. It rained all the time we were taking it back from the hulk, and now with this long passage it got heated, and there was another case of spontaneous combustion.

"The captain called us into the cabin. He had a chart spread on the table, and looked unhappy. He said, 'The coast of West Australia is near, but I mean to proceed to our destination. It is the hurricane month, too; but we will just keep her head for Bankok, and fight the fire. No more putting back anywhere, if we all get roasted. We will try first to stifle this 'ere damned combustion by want of air.'

"We tried. We battened down everything, and still she smoked. The smoke kept coming out through imperceptible crevices; it forced itself through bulkheads and covers; it oozed here and there and everywhere in slender threads, in an invisible film, in an incomprehensible manner. It made its way into the cabin, into the forecastle; it poisoned the sheltered places on the deck, it could be sniffed as high as the mainyard. It was clear that if the smoke came out the air came in. This was disheartening. This combustion refused to be stifled.

"We resolved to try water, and took the hatches off. Enormous volumes of smoke, whitish, yellowish, thick, greasy, misty, choking, ascended as high as the trucks. All hands cleared out aft. Then the poisonous cloud blew away, and we went back to work in a smoke that was no thicker now than that of an ordinary factory chimney.

"We rigged the force-pump, got the hose along, and by and by it burst. Well, it was as old as the ship—a prehistoric hose, and past repair. Then we pumped with the feeble head-pump, drew water with buckets, and in this way managed in time to pour lots of Indian Ocean into the main hatch. The bright stream flashed in sunshine, fell into a layer of white crawling smoke, and vanished on the black surface of coal. Steam ascended mingling with the smoke. We poured salt water as into a barrel without a bottom. It was our fate to pump in that ship, to pump out of her, to pump into her; and after keeping water out of her to save ourselves from being drowned, we frantically poured water into her to save ourselves from being burnt.

"And she crawled on, do or die, in the serene weather. The sky was a miracle of purity, a miracle of azure. The sea was polished, was blue, was pellucid, was sparkling like a precious stone, extending on all sides, all round to the horizon—as if the whole terrestrial globe had been one jewel, one colossal sapphire, a single gem fashioned into a planet. And on the lustre of the great calm waters the *Judea* glided imperceptibly, enveloped in languid and unclean vapours, in a lazy cloud that drifted to leeward, light and slow; a pestiferous cloud defiling the splendour of sea and sky.

"All this time of course we saw no fire. The cargo smouldered at the bottom somewhere. Once Mahon, as we were working side by side, said to me with a queer smile: 'Now, if she only would spring a tidy leak—like that time when we first left the Channel—it would put a stopper on this fire. Wouldn't it?' I remarked irrelevantly, 'Do you remember the rats?'

"We fought the fire and sailed the ship too as carefully as though nothing had been the matter. The steward cooked and attended to us. Of the other twelve men, eight worked while four rested. Everyone took his turn, captain included. There was equality, and if not exactly fraternity, then a deal of good feeling. Sometimes a man, as he dashed a bucketful of water down the hatchway, would yell out, 'Hurrah for Bankok!' and the rest laughed. But generally we were taciturn and serious—and thirsty. Oh! how thirsty! And we had to be careful with the water. Strict allowance. The ship smoked, the sun blazed . . . . Pass the bottle.

"We tried everything. We even made an attempt to dig down to the fire. No good, of course. No man could remain more than a minute below. Mahon, who went first, fainted there, and the man who went to fetch him out did likewise. We lugged them out on deck. Then I leaped down to show how easily it could be done. They had learned wisdom by that time, and contented themselves by fishing for me with a chain-hook tied to a broomhandle, I believe: I did not offer to go and fetch my shovel, which was left down below.

"Things began to look bad. We put the long-boat into the water. The second boat was ready to swing out. We had also another, a 14-foot thing, on davits aft, where it was quite safe.

"Then, behold, the smoke suddenly decreased. We redoubled our efforts to flood the bottom of the ship. In two days there was no smoke at all. Everybody was on the broad grin. This was on a Friday. On Saturday no work, but sailing the ship of course, was done. The men washed their clothes and their faces for the first time in a fortnight, and had a special dinner given them. They spoke of spontaneous combustion with contempt, and implied *they* were the boys to put out combustions. Somehow we all felt as though we each had inherited a large fortune. But a beastly smell of burning hung about the ship. Captain Beard had hollow eyes and sunken cheeks. I had never noticed so much before how twisted and bowed he was. He and Mahon prowled soberly about hatches and ventilators, sniffing. It struck me suddenly poor Mahon was a very, very old chap. As to me, I was as pleased and proud as though I had helped to win a great naval battle. O! Youth!

"The night was fine. In the morning a homeward-bound ship passed us hull down—the first we had seen for months; but we were nearing the land at last, Java Head being about 190 miles off, and nearly due north.

"Next day it was my watch on deck from eight to twelve. At breakfast the captain observed, 'It's wonderful how that smell hangs about the cabin.' About ten, the mate being on the poop, I stepped down on the main-deck for a moment. The carpenter's bench stood abaft the mainmast: I leaned against it sucking at my pipe, and the carpenter, a young chap, came to talk to me. He remarked, 'I think we have done very well, haven't we?' and then I perceived with annoyance the fool was trying to tilt the bench. I said curtly, 'Don't, Chips,' and immediately became aware of a queer sensation, of an absurd delusion,—I seemed somehow to be in the air. I heard all round me like a pent-up breath released—as if a thousand giants simultaneously had said Phoo!—and felt a dull concussion which made my ribs ache suddenly. No doubt about it—I was in the air, and my body was describing a short parabola. But short as it was, I had the time to think several thoughts in, as far as I can remember, the following order: 'This can't be the carpenter—What is it?— Some accident—Submarine volcano?—Coals, gas!—By Jove! we are being blown up—Everybody's dead—I am falling into the after-hatch—I see fire in it.'

"The coal-dust suspended in the air of the hold had glowed dull-red at the moment of the explosion. In the twinkling of an eye, in an infinitesimal fraction of a second since the first tilt of the bench, I was sprawling full length on the cargo. I picked myself up and scrambled out. It was quick like a rebound. The deck was a wilderness of smashed timber, lying crosswise like trees in a wood after a hurricane; an immense curtain of soiled rags waved gently before me—it was the mainsail blown to strips. I thought, The masts will be toppling over directly; and to get out of the way bolted on all-fours towards the poop-ladder. The first person I saw was Mahon, with eyes like saucers, his mouth open, and the long white hair standing straight on end round his head like a silver halo. He was just about to go down when the sight of the main-deck stirring, heaving up, and changing into splinters before his eyes, petrified him on the top step. I stared at him in unbelief, and he stared at me with a queer kind of shocked curiosity. I did not know that I had no hair, no eyebrows, no eyelashes, that my young moustache was burnt off, that my face was black, one cheek laid open, my nose cut, and my chin bleeding. I had lost my cap, one of my slippers, and my shirt was torn to rags. Of all this I was not aware. I was amazed to see the ship still afloat, the poop-deck whole—and, most of all, to see anybody alive. Also the peace of the sky and the serenity of the sea were distinctly surprising. I suppose I expected to see them convulsed with horror. . . .

from **The Sun Also Rises** *by Ernest Hemingway, published by Charles Scribner's Sons*

The stretch of ground from the edge of the town to the bull-ring was muddy. There was a crowd all along the fence that led to the ring, and the outside balconies and the top of the bull-ring were solid with people. I heard the rocket and I knew I could not get into the ring in time to see the bulls come in, so I shoved through the crowd to the fence. I was pushed close against the planks of the fence. Between the two fences of the runway the police were clearing the crowd along. They walked or trotted on into the bull-ring. Then people commenced to come running. A drunk slipped and fell. Two policemen grabbed him and rushed him over to the fence. The crowd were running fast now. There was a great shout from the crowd, and putting my head through between the boards I saw the bulls just coming out of the street into the long running pen. They were going fast and gaining on the crowd. Just then another drunk started out from the fence with a blouse in his hands. He wanted to do capework with the bulls. The two policemen tore out, collared him, one hit him with a club, and they dragged him against the fence and stood flattened out against the fence as the last of the crowd and the bulls went by. There were so many people running ahead of the bulls that the mass thickened and slowed up going through the gate into the ring, and as the bulls passed, galloping together, heavy, muddy-sided, horns swinging, one shot ahead, caught a man in the running crowd in the back and lifted him in the air. Both the man's arms were by his sides, his head went back as the horn went in, and the bull lifted him and then dropped him. The bull picked another man running in front, but the man disappeared into the crowd, and the crowd was through the gate and into the ring with the bulls behind them. The red door of the ring went shut, the crowd on the outside balconies of the bull-ring were pressing through to the inside, there was a shout, then another shout.

The man who had been gored lay face down in the trampled mud. People climbed over the fence, and I could not see the man because the crowd was so thick around him. From inside the ring came the shouts. Each shout meant a charge by some bull into the crowd. You could tell by the degree of intensity in the shout how bad a thing it was that was happening. Then the rocket went up that meant the steers had gotten the bulls out of the ring and into the corrals. I left the fence and started back toward the town.

Back in the town I went to the café to have a second coffee and some buttered toast. The waiters were sweeping out the café and mopping off the tables. One came over and took my order.

"Anything happen at the encierro?"

"I didn't see it all. One man was badly cogido."

"Where?"

"Here." I put one hand on the small of my back and the other on my chest, where it looked as though the horn must have come through. The waiter nodded his head and swept the crumbs from the table with his cloth.

"Badly cogido," he said. "All for sport. All for pleasure."

He went away and came back with the long-handled coffee and milk pots. He poured the milk and coffee. It came out of the long spouts in two streams into the big cup. The waiter nodded his head.

"Badly cogido through the back," he said. He put the pots down on the table and sat down in the chair at the table. "A big horn wound. All for fun. Just for fun. What do you think of that?"

"I don't know."

"That's it. All for fun. Fun, you understand."

"You're not an aficionado?"

"Me? What are bulls? Animals. Brute animals." He stood up and put his hand on the small of his back. "Right through the back. A cornada right through the back. For fun—you understand."

He shook his head and walked away, carrying the coffee-pots. Two men were going by in the street. The waiter shouted to them. They were grave-looking. One shook his head. "Muerto!" he called.

The waiter nodded his head. The two men went on. They were on some errand. The waiter came over to my table.

"You hear? Muerto. Dead. He's dead. With a horn through him. All for morning fun. Es muy flamenco."

"It's bad."

"Not for me," the waiter said. "No fun in that for me."

Later in the day we learned that the man who was killed was named Vicente Girones, and came from near Tafalla. The next day in the paper we read that he was twenty-eight years old, and had a farm, a wife, and two children. He had continued to come to the fiesta each year after he was married. The next day his wife came in from Tafalla to be with the body, and the day after there was a service in the chapel of San Fermin, and the coffin was carried to the railway-station by members of the dancing and drinking society of Tafalla. The drums marched ahead, and there was music on the fifes, and behind the men who carried the coffin walked the wife and two children . . . . Behind them marched all the members of the dancing and drinking societies of Pamplona, Estella, Tafalla, and Sanguesa who could stay over for the funeral. The coffin was loaded into the baggage-car of the train, and the widow and the two children rode, sitting, all three together, in an open third-class railway-carriage. The train started with a jerk, and then ran smoothly, going down grade around the edge of the plateau and out into the fields of grain that blew in the wind on the plain on the way to Tafalla.

chapter 13

STYLE AND TONE

STYLE DEFINED

Style is the manner of expression which distinguishes one piece of writing from another. It is *how* a writer uses the language. For purposes of analysis, we can discuss style as if it were distinct from the subject matter, but keep in mind that style and content are as intermeshed and interdependent as rhythm and melody in music.

All writing has style, just as all speech has an accent. What is sometimes called "no-accent" by those in broadcasting is simply the accent of the majority at a particular point in history. In the same way, some stories and novels do not have a readily identifiable style because they are in the mainstream of contemporary fiction. If you read carefully, however, you will find that the work of most major writers can be identified by certain recurring characteristics. Like handwriting, these stylistic patterns can be subtle or highly distinctive.

Having a distinctive style is not in itself "good" or "bad." But when we can identify a writer's particular style it adds to our pleasure just as it does in music when we can hear exactly what makes one artist's work different from all others.

ELEMENTS OF STYLE

There are three major elements which determine prose style in fiction: *diction* (word choice), *syntax* (sentence structure), and the *balance of narrative modes*. Each deserves a close look.

Diction

Word choice is a particularly important factor in English because this language has an enormous vocabulary—far larger, for example, than French, German, or Spanish. It's roots are both Germanic (Anglo-Saxon) and classical (Greek and Latin). In addition, it has absorbed words from a great variety of other languages including Eskimo (kayak, igloo), Chinese (tong, gong, tea) and American Indian (tepee, papoose). As a result of all this amalgamation we often have two or even three words which mean basically the same thing. But because their roots are different, they usually have different overtones. *Car,* for example, sounds less elegant than *automobile. Boat* is simpler than *vessel* not just because of the length of the word but also because quite unconsciously we think of Anglo-Saxon and Old Norse words as being simple or even crude and words with a classical origin as being more refined. (Be careful about these prejudices when you write papers, however. A straightforward style using the correct word, not the fanciest, is preferred today.)

You will not want to interrupt your reading to look up a large number of derivations, but from time to time take a close look at the words which are being used. The style of Ernest Hemingway, for example, which is represented in the previous chapter, is distinctive largely because of the simple sentence structure. But his word choice is also a factor. He avoids Latinate roots where possible. In that passage he uses "grabbed" instead of "seized," "drunk" instead of "intoxicated." To some degree, these words are closer to those we use in conversation. By way of contrast, in the excerpt from *Youth* (also included in the previous chapter) Joseph Conrad uses an entirely different approach. The scene is equally dramatic—an explosion at sea—but Conrad's word choice is far less conversational, as seen in phrases like, "my body was describing a short parabola" and "in an infinitesimal fraction of a second. . . ." Even without knowing the derivations of these words one can feel the difference diction can make in the tone of a work.

Diction is a particularly important factor in any type of dialogue. Spoken language is relatively informal, so in order to catch this flavor in fiction most authors use colloquial words and an occasional slang expression when writing dialogue. These reflect not only the character and background of the fictional speaker but the historical period as well.

When a story or novel is written in the first person as if it were being narrated aloud, this informality extends to the entire work. John Updike, for example, normally writes with a more extensive vocabulary than many authors. He seems to enjoy using words which are not frequently heard in conversation. But you would never guess this from reading "A & P." In that story he adopts the diction of a young man working in a supermarket. The style is not as rambling and disjointed as a tape recording would be, but the narrator refers to groceries as "goodies," the hair of one of the girls as "sort of oaky," and uses "pipes up" for "speaks." There are not many of these colloquial expressions, but just enough to give the flavor of someone like Sammy talking out loud.

Joseph Conrad's *Youth* is also a narrated story, which may seem surprising at first in view of the somewhat elevated diction he uses. But don't forget that the manner of daily speech at the turn of the century, when *Youth* was written, was not the same as it is today. In addition, the narrator is an older man recalling the events of his youth.

When analyzing the diction of a story or novel, consider the historical period of the writing and the stylistic inclinations of the author. If the work is written in the first person as if it were narrated aloud, consider the age and character of the fictional speaker as well.

Style is also affected by the use of such devices as *similes, metaphors,* and *symbols.* In a sense, these can be considered as aspects of diction. But they are a topic of their own and are included under the general heading of *heightened language* in the next chapter.

Syntax

The term *syntax* includes not only the length of the sentences but their construction. In order to describe the way sentence structure affects a particular author's style, it is very helpful to be familiar with some basic grammatical terms. A "simple sentence," for example, is one which contains one subject and one verb. "The ship sank." is a simple sentence. When a prose passage has a high percentage of simple sentences, the effect seems stark and unadorned. It can have great power, but if the technique is pushed too far, the style may become "choppy."

A "compound sentence" links two independent clauses (a group of words containing a subject and a verb) with a conjunction like *and* or *but* or with a semicolon—for example, "The ship sank, and many lives were lost." Essentially, this is like two simple sentences joined with a conjunction or appropriate punctuation.

A third grammatical unit is the "complex sentence." This has a main clause just like the simple sentence and a dependent clause—one which depends on the main clause to complete its meaning: "The ship sank when it struck an iceberg."

When prose is written with compound and complex sentences, the style can, if handled skillfully, seem to flow more smoothly. There comes a point, however, when such sentences may seem cluttered and lacking in force. It is up to each author to judge what length and type is the most effective for a particular passage. Sentence structure and length, therefore, depend on a number of factors: the demands of an individual scene, the general preferences of the author, and the influence of the historical period in which the author lives.

When describing an author's style, watch out for phrases like "seems to flow more smoothly" or "choppy." Sometimes they are necessary, but they are vague and rather subjective. One reader's "choppy" style may seem "forceful and compelling" to another. Whatever judgment you make, identify it as opinion with phrases like "it appears to me" and then support your view with specific reference to the type of syntax being used.

There is another distinction which is particularly helpful when analyzing fiction written previous to our own century. The *periodic sentence* is one in which the full meaning is not completed until the end. "The ship, which struck an iceberg, sank" is "periodic" in the sense that it is not complete until the period. Notice how our earlier version, "The ship sank when it struck an iceberg," is grammatically complete with the word "sank." That is called a "non-periodic" or "loose" sentence.

Periodic sentences often have more force because the verb comes at the end, but they can sound somewhat formal or even stiff. Here, for example, is a nonperiodic and conversationally natural sentence: "The ship sank because it was traveling at full speed when it hit the berg." Converted to a periodic sentence it would read like this: "Because the ship was traveling at full speed when it hit the berg, it sank."

Modification also influences the way a sentence "sounds" and so affects the style. When looking at the adjectives and adverbs, consider how many are used (density), where they are placed, and whether they are conversational or somewhat unusual. If we go back to our first sentence, "The ship sank," we can alter the style simply with modifiers: "The famous ship sank quickly," for example, is conventional and close to what we might say in conversation. Compare it with, "The ship—proud, famous, but sadly vulnerable—sank forthwith." The meaning is essentially the same, but the style is quite different. Notice the changes in order (adjectives placed after the noun), density (three more adjectives), and type (more formal). There is a certain elegance in the second version, but by contemporary standards, it sounds a bit stilted. That judgment, like most matters of style, is ultimately a matter of taste.

If you apply these syntactical distinctions to the two samples of fiction in the previous chapter, you will be able to describe in fairly precise terms how they differ in style. The selection by Hemingway is dominated by simple sentences. Although the second and third are compound sentences, the next seven are simple. Modifiers are kept to a minimum. This rather stark, simple style is one which Hemingway often adopted. There are occasions when he departed from it for effect, but not many.

Although the selection from Joseph Conrad's *Youth* also begins with some simple sentences, it is soon dominated by more complex constructions. In addition, his modifiers are more profuse. This is not entirely due to the fact that he was writing at the turn of the century. You can find contemporary examples of relatively complex syntax in the works of such authors as William Faulkner and Saul Bellow.

Novelists in the eighteenth and nineteenth centuries tended to have a certain fondness for relatively complex syntactical constructions, and occasionally they seemed to use them just for fun, the way a jazz player today might enjoy a complex improvisation. The following example is taken from *Vanity Fair* by William Thackeray (1848). It is an extreme example (with some very odd punctuation), but it represents the other end of the spectrum from the sample by Hemingway. Dobbin is the subject of this sentence and he is anxious to be on the road back to London:

> Although the sight of that magnificent round of beef, and the silver tankard suggestive of real British home-brewed ale and porter, which perennially greet the eyes of the traveller returning from foreign parts, who enters the coffee-room of the "George," are so invigorating and delightful, that a man entering such a comfortable snug homely English inn, might well like to stop some days there, yet Dobbin began to talk about a post-chaise instantly, and was no sooner at Southampton than he wished to be on the road to London.

The balance of narrative modes

The concept of narrative modes was introduced in the chapter on characterization. It is equally important in the examination of literary style.

To review quickly, every sentence of a story or novel can be described as being cast predominantly in one of these five modes: dialogue, thought, action, description, or exposition. Most fiction is made up of a balance of these modes, shifting from those which are static (description and exposition) to those which are more active, and then back again. If an author concentrates on one at the expense of the others, the style will be radically affected.

Stressing dialogue as the dominant narrative mode tends to make a work of fiction looser, more informal, and less structured. This is true even when the work is written in the third person. J. D. Salinger's frequently anthologized story, "Uncle Wiggily in Connecticut," is a good illustration. It reads almost like a radio script. Another example is his novel, *Franny and Zooey*. Characterization in works like these is achieved not as much by action as by the dialogue itself.

An as-if-narrated story is an extreme example of fiction which is dominated by dialogue—unless the speaker's identity becomes lost as the work progresses. A story like "A & P" is carefully composed as fiction by the author, but it gives the impression of a personal experience being told in conversation. It *sounds* spontaneous to us even though the author has planned the structure carefully.

Quite a different effect is achieved when action and thoughts are stressed and dialogue is cut to a minimum. Ernest Hemingway's short novel, *The Old Man and the Sea,* is a good example. Since the fisherman in that work has a long, solitary ordeal in his boat, the author devotes a great deal of attention to his thoughts. The character also talks out loud to himself, but these passages are more like thoughts than true dialogue. Whenever a work of fiction is based on a single character who is in some way isolated, the natural tendency is to stress that character's inner life through his or her thoughts.

We tend to think of "action-packed" fiction as being simple: spy novels, tales of adventure, murder, and intrigue. Yet Langston Hughes' story "On the Road" depends almost entirely on action, and it is in no way simple. In stressing the events (action), Hughes makes little use of thoughts, dialogue, or exposition. We don't know much about what is going on in Sargeant's mind (though we can guess), and we are not told how to interpret the events. Action tells it all, and what it suggests about poverty, race, and religion in America today is highly complex.

Much of what you read balances the five modes in a way which does not affect the style in any radical way. But be sure to examine a sample page carefully. If the writing seems to make unusual use of one particular mode, check other sections of the work to see if this is a sustained pattern. If it is, try to judge what influence it has on the overall effect.

When you look at the characteristic patterns of diction, syntax, and the use of narrative modes, you are beginning to identify what makes a particular author's style distinctive. Knowing this will help you to see more in whatever work you are reading, and it will provide a kind of introduction to the next title by the same author.

Keep this in mind when reading fiction written in previous centuries. Resist the inclination to judge these works as if they should have been written in the style of the twentieth century. Each age has its own stylistic pattern, and within each of those traditions individual authors add their own imprint. There are infinite variations. Read with an open mind.

TONE

Tone is the attitude an author or a narrator takes toward the material and toward his or her audience. We describe tone in literature in much the same way as we do tone of voice: as formal or informal, serious or comic, ironic or literal, satiric or nonsatiric, and the like.

This initial definition, paraphrased from the critic I. A. Richards, is a good starting point for what can be a rather complex subject. The complexity comes from the fact that although tone is enormously important, it is often subtle and open to question. We face this even in daily speech: "Was she serious?" someone asks. "No, she was only kidding." An important difference of opinion there. "Is he really arguing for an end to social security payments?" "Of course not, he was being highly ironic." These simple examples indicate how the very meaning of a spoken statement can occasionally depend on how we interpret the speaker's tone.

If meaning depends so heavily on tone in daily conversation, it is no wonder that we have to look very closely at the subtleties of tone in literature. Tone is far more than just an adornment to fiction; it is often a necessary key to understanding the intent of the work as a whole.

Formal versus informal

The tone of some works can be said to be relatively *formal* and others more *informal*. There are many gradations between the two extremes, of course. We have already seen how the language (diction and syntax) of the story "A & P" is more informal than that of Conrad's work *Youth,* even though both are as-if-narrated. Informality in fiction is achieved by adopting both the diction and the syntax of conversation, and this can be done both in first- and third-person writing. Good examples include Richard Fariña's *Been Down So Long It Looks Like Up to Me* and most of the novels by Tom Robbins and Kurt Vonnegut. Popular as the informal tone is in contemporary fiction, there is no evidence that it is taking over. Novels by such major authors as Margaret Drabble, John Updike, Gail Godwin, and Saul Bellow maintain a verbal standard which is far more formal without in any way losing wide appeal.

Serious versus comic

Usually we can all agree as to what is serious and what is comic. But not always. There are some terrible events in Joseph Heller's *Catch 22* which some readers see as grim and others as grotesquely funny. The short stories of Roald Dahl and Nathanael West's novel *Miss Lonelyhearts* also present readers with this dilemma. This is sometimes referred to as *black humor,* a term which does not indicate fiction by black writers but comedy which is so dark that we are sometimes uncertain as to whether we should laugh or be horrified. To avoid confusion, it might more accurately be called *bitter comedy.*

When we speak of comic tones, it is often helpful to make a distinction between *humor* and *wit.* Humor is generally considered to be kinder, more sympathetic. (*Black humor* is an odd exception.) Wit, on the other hand, is generally considered to be sharper, more critical, sometimes biting. The distinction between humor and wit is especially helpful when deciding exactly what tone an author has used in presenting a particular character. Sammy, the protagonist in "A & P," for example, is treated with sympathetic humor. If that story were highly satiric—ridiculing both major characters—the tone would be considered wit, not humor.

Ironic tone

Irony is closely associated with wit. We are all familiar with *verbal irony* because it is similar to what we call "sarcasm" in daily speech. Essentially it is a matter of a character's or the author's using some form of understatement or, less often, overstatement for effect. If, for example, a police officer sees half the town washed away in a flash flood and says, "We've got a problem here," we know from the tone that he or she is speaking ironically (understatement) and is not being indifferent. Or let us suppose a husband has gone into a tirade because his wife has come home ten minutes late from a meeting and she says, "So shoot me." We know that she has used overstatement for effect—and he'd better not take her literally!

Sometimes an ironic line is easy to miss on first reading because we don't have enough information at that point to interpret the tone. There is an example of this in "Small Point Bridge." When Isaac Bates, the protagonist, finally gets around to the real reason he has come to see his old associate, Seth, he says, "There's a small matter I don't want to forget." He knows perfectly well that it is not a "small matter," and although you have no way of seeing the irony just then, you soon find out. In that same scene it becomes clear that the "small matter" is crucial to them both, an irony which is echoed in the title, "Small Point Bridge."

In this example, the irony is limited to what a character says. It is possible, however, to write an entire work of fiction with an ironic tone. This is found more frequently in short stories than in novels. It usually takes the form of a naive protagonist who does not understand how significant the experience really is. One of the finest examples of this is a relatively long story by Peter Taylor called "A Spinster's Tale." As the title suggests, the narrator is a spinster. Through her own story we learn what she herself has never understood: that all her life she has been dealing with a repressed fear of men and sex. Notice that in this case the narrator is completely unaware of the irony. But the *story* is highly ironic in that it reveals so much more about her than she understands.

With all types of verbal irony, it is helpful to distinguish the *literal statement* from the *intended meaning*. The greater the contrast, the sharper the irony.

There is another type of irony which is sometimes called *cosmic irony* or *irony of fate*. Here the reversal is in events or physical details rather than narration. This kind of irony is not associated with wit; in fact, it is frequently grim. In Langston Hughes' story "On the Road," for example, there is an ironic contrast between the protagonist, a black man, and the white snow which at first he didn't even see. For emphasis, the snow is described as sticking to his "black hands." Shortly after that, the steps to the all-white church are described as "all snowy white." In terms of tone, sharp ironic contrasts like this often reflect some degree of bitterness.

Satiric tone

Closely associated with irony is *satire*. Satire is a special form of wit in which a distorted view of characters, places, or institutions is used to ridicule and criticize the subject. There is always some degree of exaggeration, though in some cases it may come only from which details are selected and which are omitted. Since there is a pretense that the distorted version is the truth, satire is always presented with a kind of irony. It is rather like the irony of a comedian who keeps a straight face. This is what distinguishes satire from direct criticism.

Many of us were introduced to a rather blunt type of satire in *Mad* and later in *The National Lampoon*. Also, satiric skits are always popular on television. But literary satire can be far more ingenious and clever (as in the satiric works of Evelyn Waugh, for example) and far more subtle (as in the novels of J. P. Marquand). In this volume, there are samples of gentle satire in John Updike's story "A & P." Both the narrator and the supermarket are viewed in a subtly comic manner.

When a literary style is satirized, the result is called a *parody*. The author selects the primary characteristics of the style and exaggerates them with comic effect.

EXAMINING STYLE AND TONE

With many short stories, you may wish to postpone a close examination of style and tone until you have finished. When reading novels, on the other hand, be sure to stop after the first chapter to take a close look at both of these aspects. In either case, write out your impressions in the form of brief notes. The act of writing will help to focus your attention.

Is there, for example, anything distinctive about the author's word choice? What influence has the sentence structure on the overall effect? Has any one of the five narrative modes been stressed at the expense of the others?

Then see if you can describe briefly the tone of the work. Is the writing formal or informal, serious or comic? If comic, would you characterize it as having the warmth of humor or the sparkle and perhaps the bite of wit? Are there samples of irony either in the dialogue of the characters or in the approach taken by the author? Are there satiric elements?

TOPICS FOR ANALYSIS

If you are planning to write a short paper on this subject, you might want to consider one of these topics:

1. Select a paragraph of description by an author writing previous to 1900. (Consider Charles Dickens, George Eliot, William Thackery, for example; or find a short story from an anthology.) Photocopy (or copy) that one paragraph. Underline the words and phrases which seem different from those a contemporary writer might use. Then rewrite the passage using a contemporary style (both diction and syntax) while at the same time staying as close to the original as you can.

2. Select two works which are significantly different in style. (Look through an anthology, examining sample paragraphs. Or consider any sample page by such contrasting stylists as Henry James and Ernest Hemingway or Kurt Vonnegut and John Updike.) Then analyze exactly how they differ. Be as specific as you can. (Consider diction, syntax, narrative modes.) Quote passages to illustrate your analysis.

3. Select a paragraph of fiction by an author who is not a pronounced stylist. (John Knowles, William Styron, and Gail Godwin are all good examples.) Photocopy (or copy) the paragraph. Now write a new version in which you combine as many sentences as you can. Add at least five modifiers (adjectives or adverbs). Then analyze how the tone of the paragraph has changed.

4. Select a page of fiction by an author with a distinctive style. (William Faulkner, Henry James, Tom Robbins, Ernest Hemingway, Richard Fariña, and Charles Dickens are all good examples.) Photocopy (or copy) that page. Then write a short *parody*—that is, revise the situation and adopt a style which is a slight exaggeration of your model. Parody is good fun, but it is also a highly effective way of studying an author's style.

Whether you write a formal paper or merely jot down some notes on the style and tone of a work you have just finished, you will find that the act of getting something down on paper is well worth your time. It is all too easy to read fiction with plot and character in mind, letting the subtleties of style slip by you like background music. When passive readers describe a story or novel they have read with the cliché "Well, it's different," what they usually mean is that the style is distinctive but they aren't sure how to describe what those distinctions are. They have missed a good deal.

If you take the time to describe to yourself exactly what makes a work of fiction different in terms of style and tone, you can be sure that you have drawn full value and pleasure from your reading.

chapter 14

HEIGHTENED LANGUAGE: SIMILE, METAPHOR, AND SYMBOL

direct comparisons contrasted with figures of speech: similes and metaphors, irony, hyperbole, personification
allegory as an extended form of metaphor
symbolic details: examining figurative and symbolic elements
heightened awareness
topics for analysis

FIGURES OF SPEECH

Similes, metaphors, and symbols are all ways of heightening or intensifying language. They make a few words suggest a lot more than their literal meaning.

This is an important point because it helps to guard against two misconceptions. The first is that similes, metaphors, and symbols are limited to highly sophisticated literary works. Actually they are found in the language of children, the oral literature of nonliterate societies, and the verbal outpouring of our own pop culture—the world of ads, commercials, and song lyrics.

The second misconception is that such devices are merely stylistic decorations. While it is true that they are elements of style, like all elements of style they can also serve as important or even essential aspects of the meaning itself. They actually make language do more than it can on a literal level.

Similes and metaphors

Both similes and metaphors are comparisons. What makes them different from conventional comparisons is that the object or action being described is likened to something essentially *dissimilar* in all ways but one.

For example, here is a simple comparison: "The sea was as calm as a lake at dawn." The two objects are essentially the same. But here is that same picture of tranquility presented through a simile: "The sea was as calm as a sleeping cat." We don't for a minute visualize a sea with fur and whiskers. Quite unconsciously we focus on that one area of similarity, the sense of perfect calm.

A metaphor works in essentially the same way except that the comparison is made without the word *like* or *as*. That same scene could be described metaphorically this way: "The sea was a great sleeping cat." We're not tempted to read this literally as if it were some wild bit of science fiction because, being used to metaphors in print and even in daily speech, we translate the statement quite unconsciously, just as we do a simile.

The difference between similes and metaphors may seem at first like a mere matter of grammar, but actually there is more to it than that. The metaphor is stronger, more vivid. Can you feel the difference in these two examples?

> "She was like a tiger when she defended her children."
> "She was a tiger defending her children."

In order to understand how similes and metaphors work, it helps to see them as belonging to a group of devices called *figures of speech*. A figure of speech (also called figurative language) is any phrase which departs from its literal meaning to create a special effect. In most cases, the literal meaning is actually untrue; what we respond to is a figurative or implied meaning. In the example just given, for example, the sea was not *literally* like a cat, but we can say that it was *figuratively* like a cat.

Irony

If you keep in mind that both similes and metaphors are types of figurative language, you will see how they are related to other figures of speech such as *irony*. In the previous chapter I explained how irony also has a literal meaning which may be entirely untrue, as in the case of a person in a hurricane who says, "Great day for a sail."

Hyperbole

Another figure of speech is *hyperbole*, extreme exaggeration used for effect. Andrew Marvel, for example, refers to his love as "vaster than empires." On a more prosaic level we might describe an active five year old as a "tornado." Only the most literal-minded person would dive for the storm cellar!

Personification

Another closely related figure of speech is *personification*, investing objects or ideas with human characteristics. "Mother Earth" is a conventionalized and overused personification. "The Sahara is a thirsty land" is less common. Sometimes personification is merely hinted at in a description. "The wind clawed at her face" and "The city slept in the noon heat" are based on implied personifications.

Each of these different figures of speech—simile, metaphor, irony, hyperbole, personification—have two things in common: They each have a literal meaning which we skip over almost unconsciously, and they each have a figurative or implied meaning. In most cases, we understand the intent without stopping to analyze the two elements, but that understanding is greater when we examine how the process works.

Fiction often contains figures of speech—particularly similes and metaphors—because one of its goals is to give you strong visual impressions and a sense of sharing a particular human experience. Factual writing usually contains fewer, though the nature articles in magazines like *The National Geographic* and *Scientific American* make occasional use of them. Business reports and legal documents quite rightly avoid such language altogether because in that type of writing accuracy and precision are more important than vividness.

But this does not mean that all fiction contains figurative language. Or that it should. The selection from Ernest Hemingway's novel *The Sun Also Rises* is a good example. In that particular section, there is not a single simile or metaphor. There are a few in the novel as a whole, but not many. The author tends to avoid both figurative language and abstract analysis and relies instead on clear, concrete details. The result is highly visual— almost like a film clip.

Joseph Conrad also creates highly visual scenes, but he prefers to use both direct comparisons and figurative language. Here are some examples taken from the passage beginning on page 89. I have italicized the portion of each quotation which is a simple comparison, a simile, or a metaphor.

> "The smell down below was as unexpected as it was frightful. One would have thought *hundreds of paraffin-lamps had been flaring and smoking in that hold for days.*"

This is a simple comparison, not a simile, because all those smoky lamps would have created a scene quite literally like the one he is describing.

> "We poured salt water *as into a barrel without a bottom.*"

This is a true simile since the ship was not literally a barrel without a bottom.

> "The sea . . . was sparkling *like a precious stone,* extending on all sides, all round to the horizon—*as if the whole terrestrial globe had been one jewel, one colossal sapphire, a single gem fashioned into a planet.*"

This is a simile which has been extended and amplified.

"The sky was *a miracle of purity, a miracle of azure.*"

This is a metaphor because the author states that the sky *was* a miracle, not was *like* one. It is also an hyperbole—an exaggeration used for effect. Unfortunately, the word *miracle* has since been so overused as a popular hyperbole (as in "miracle drugs") that today it has lost much of its original impact.

It is natural enough to miss a number of similes and metaphors when you read a work of fiction for the first time. Most authors try to keep them from standing out too blatantly because they want to achieve an effect without making the reader aware of the technique. The time to look at them analytically is in your second reading or when you review the work. You will find that each author has a somewhat different approach to the use of figurative language.

ALLEGORY

An *allegory* is really an extended form of metaphor. In an allegory, all the characters in a story, novel, or a narrative poem take on strong and consistent metaphorical meaning. In most cases, their abstract meaning becomes more important than their human attributes.

One of the most famous examples in prose is John Bunyon's *Pilgrim's Progress*. The hero is called Christian and he deals with characters like Mr. Worldly-Wiseman, Sloth, Presumption, and Mr. Good-will. His adventures take Christian to such places as the Valley of the Shadow of Death, the Slough of Despond, and Vanity Fair. The work seems a bit naive to us now, but in many nineteenth-century homes it ranked second only to the Bible.

Allegories almost always have some specific message and so tend to be more concerned with theme than with characterization. In our own century the subject matter is more often political than religious. The most popular example is *Animal Farm* by George Orwell. In this work a group of barnyard animals take over a farm with mixed results, and the story becomes a biting political satire of the Soviet Union just after the Revolution.

Allegories often make use of personification—not just as a passing reference as in the examples given earlier, but as a consistent identity. In *Animal Farm,* for example, each animal represents a particular group in Soviet society. On the surface, such novels resemble children's stories; but their meaning is extended and heightened through what is essentially a complex and sustained metaphor.

SYMBOLIC DETAILS

Symbols have the reputation of being the preoccupation of English teachers. To some degree this is justified because discussing them in class is an effective way of analyzing certain literary works in depth. It is a good idea, however, to place them in perspective. On the one hand, it is perfectly possible to understand and enjoy a good deal of most literary works without being fully aware of all the symbolic details; the presence of symbols does not in itself make a work of fiction great, nor does the lack of them make it inferior. On the other hand, when there are symbolic elements in a story or novel, they can give you a far deeper understanding of that work and also a great deal of pleasure.

A symbol is any detail—an object, action, or state—which has a range of meaning beyond and usually larger than its literal definition. The word *dove*, for example, refers to a particular type of bird. It has also come to stand for or represent peace and those who favor a policy of arms reduction. In the same way, *hawk* has a literal meaning (also called *denotation*) of a more aggressive type of bird, and in addition it has come to suggest those who support an arms buildup. We distinguish the denotative meaning of these words from their symbolic meaning largely by the context. If we read in the paper that the local zoo was given a hawk, we assume this is a bird and not a politician. But if we are reading about a debate in the House of Representatives in which "Doves and hawks were in total disagreement," we don't ask what all those birds were doing in the halls of Congress.

Symbols on this level are easy to identify, fairly simple, and widely accepted. They are often used by political cartoonists. We all know that the flag can be used to represent the country, a ship as the "ship of state," the cross as the Christian church, and a tall figure called Uncle Sam as the United States. These are somewhat hackneyed symbols, but they serve a purpose.

There are also a wide range of symbols borrowed from the seasons and nature generally. Spring suggests birth, winter death. The rose has been used for several centuries to represent beauty, and the goat from Greek mythology (Pan) has been used through the ages to symbolize sexual energy.

These are called *public symbols* because they are recognized by the public at large. Occasionally they are seen in literature (such as Robert Coover's use of Uncle Sam as a major character in his novel *The Public Burning*). But the more common ones are generally avoided in fiction as being essentially clichés. Instead, authors tend to create fresh symbols of their own. These are sometimes called *private symbols* in that they have been created by individual authors for use in particular works.

Names of characters and places in fiction are often given symbolic overtones. In allegories this is done blatantly. Mr. Worldly-Wiseman in the allegory *Pilgrim's Progress*, for example, is intentionally symbolic. In fact, the character is really no more than an illustrated idea. But when authors are developing a credible character in fiction, they prefer to keep the symbolic suggestions far more subtle in order to maintain credibility.

Do you remember the name of the protagonist in Carson McCullers'

"The Sojourner?" As one whose life has been turning in circles, he is appropriately called John *Ferris*, a name with overtones of a Ferris wheel often found in amusement parks. This symbolic name is used at the very beginning of the second paragraph and then is repeated at the beginning of the third and fourth paragraphs. In spite of the repetition, you may well have missed this detail on your first reading because it is not until toward the end of the story that you see the pattern of his life and can recognize the significance of his name. A passive reader may, of course, sense the connection unconsciously; but it requires active reading to see and consciously enjoy the ingenuity of symbolic details like this.

Symbols can be far more diffuse than names of characters. The entire setting in John Updike's story "A & P" has symbolic overtones. On first reading, it is natural enough to focus on Sammy, the narrator, and his admiration of the three young women. But as you look closely at the story, notice how many details about the supermarket are given. More, certainly, than are needed for the plot.

Why, for example, are there so many lengthy and often scathing descriptions of the products on the shelves: the discount records ("Tony Martin Sings or some such gunk . . . ."), the plastic toys "that fall apart when a kid looks at them . . . ," and the like? Why is the whole store described as being "like a pinball machine" and the customers as "sheep"? What is the point of that section about the way the cash register sounds?— "'Hello (*bing*) there, you (*gung*) hap-py *pee*-pul (*splat*)!'—the *splat* being the drawer flying out."

One or two of these details could be explained merely as ways of filling in the setting, helping us to see it. But the author uses so many and has, though the narrator, presented them in such an unflattering light, that the supermarket takes on implications which are larger than mere setting. It comes to suggest the least attractive aspect of the commercial world— materialism at its worst.

How this gently satiric symbol of materialism is played against an equally gentle satire of romantic idealism in Sammy is really a matter of theme, so I will return to it in the next chapter. The point here is that symbols are sometimes created by the accumulation of details, and, incidentally, that symbols don't have to be heavy, dark suggestions about the meaning of life and death: They can just as easily be lighthearted.

When names of characters and places are used symbolically, they are fairly easy to identify—at least on second reading. But sometimes symbolic elements are used in opposition with each other. We come to see their significance mainly through their contrast.

This kind of contrast is subtly employed in Langston Hughes' story "On the Road." There is no way to spot the symbolic use of color at the very beginning of that story. The opening sentence is "He was not interested in the snow." In the next sentence we learn that "Sargeant never even noticed the snow." Natural enough—he is hungry and looking for a place to stay for the night.

But the author keeps returning to that apparently unimportant detail. "He wouldn't have known it was snowing," we are told; and then, "Sargeant didn't see the snow." All these quotations come from the very first paragraph—four specific uses of "snow" or "snowing" in six sentences!

When you look at the story for the second time, you should begin to have the feeling that something may be going on here in addition to a simple description of the weather. Keeping this possibility in mind, review the second paragraph. The means of perception shifts to the minister and his awareness of the snow gives us the clue we need to see it as a possibly symbolic detail:

> The Reverend Mr. Dorset, however, saw the snow when he switched on his porch light, opened the front door of his parsonage, and found standing there before him a big black man with snow on his face, a human piece of night with snow on his face . . . .

This is when—at least on the second reading—the symbolic use of black and white should suddenly hit you. Sargeant does not think of himself as a black man in a white world at the opening of the story. All he knows is that he is cold, hungry, and out of work. But the Reverend Mr. Dorset sees the stranger at the door as a black man in a white world.

Are we reading something into this story which isn't there? Let's be cautious. So far we have a theory, but to be sure that this is really a symbolic detail and not just coincidence, it would help if we had more references. Read on.

Sure enough, in the next paragraph we read that "The big black man turned away. And even yet he didn't see the snow, walking right into it." In the paragraph after that, he sees that the steps of a church from which he had been barred had "white steps in the night all snowy white." If this were an essay, we might criticize the author for using "snow" so redundantly. But because it is fiction, we can reasonably assume that this redundancy is being used for some special effect—just as it sometimes is in poetry.

We now reach the point when Sargeant sees Christ on the crucifix. "When he looked up, the snow fell into his eyes. For the first time that night he *saw* the snow." It is at that point in the story that Sargeant sees himself as a black man in a white world. This is a story in black and white, and both colors are fully developed symbols. These symbols are not literary adornments; they are the foundation for the theme itself.

Notice how we came to that understanding. It began as just a hunch: why does the author keep using the word *snow*? Then we made a hypothesis: *maybe* a symbol is being developed. Finally we tested our theory with further reading. The conclusion we came to was based on careful reading and accumulated evidence.

This process of analysis is as important as the analysis itself. When a critic or teacher points out a literary symbol, it sometimes seems as if such details can only be detected by experts. You may find yourself turning to critical opinions as a kind of substitute for your own active exploration. Remember, though, that when symbolic details are kept subtle it is not to trick you; it is only to keep the fiction from seeming artificial and contrived. If you stop from time to time to examine details which seem to have symbolic overtones, you will soon develop your own capacity to enjoy the expanded meaning and suggestion. What may at first seem like an interruption in your reading will soon become an almost unconscious ability to see more in what you read.

So far, we have dealt with symbols which are visual. A great majority are. But symbols can be based on action as well. There is an example of this in the final scene of "Small Point Bridge." You may wish to review that section of the story (pages 64–66) before reading the following analysis.

Isaac Bates, you remember, is standing on the wooden walkway with Seth, watching the terrible damage of the ice. They are (significantly) half-way between the island which Seth hopes to own and the mainland. Isaac's efforts have been to break Seth's legal hold on that property. To do this, he must force the old man to abandon it that night and then pay rent.

Isaac resorts to force, heaving against Seth and finally raising his hand and bringing it down "hard on Seth's wrist like a cleaver." Here is the description of what followed:

> That did it. A squeal, a falling back, and a great rumbling like a line of boxcars being suddenly nudged, the sound resounding against his chest. Isaac felt a deep surge of power and then, catching sight of something larger out of the corner of his eye, turned just in time to see the whole front wall of his cannery pier buckle and slide toward the saw-tooth jumble of gray ice.

My hope is to blend the violence of Isaac with that of the winter ice, linking the destructive power of nature with that of a man who has become locked into an obsessive resolve.

The next paragraph describes the cannery falling apart. Even the filing cabinets split open and scatter "the records of a lifetime." Isaac's own life is being torn apart.

Neither Isaac nor the reader may be fully aware of the connections at this point, but the ice has become a symbol of his own power and obstinacy, and the broken cannery suggests the damage such action can do to a man's life—both his and Seth's. This is the point at which Isaac, shocked, relents and guides Seth back to the island.

In terms of plot, the story is over at that point. But sometimes it is wise to put some of the pieces together. In this case, those same symbolic connections are touched on once again. Back in the cabin Seth says, "You're a hard, cold sonofabitch." This echoes what Isaac said to the grinding ice at the beginning of the story. Seth is then described as looking "like something washed up after a storm . . . like bits and pieces from the wrecked cannery." The symbolic connection finally breaks through on Isaac himself. He wonders with alarm: "Had he spent a lifetime on that miserable coast only to end up harsh as the sea itself?"

The story closes not with a symbol but a simile. The two men have been drawn together in friendship once again, and Isaac sings ballads "which he had known as a boy and which had lain dormant in him like seeds through the course of a long, hard winter."

Is it essential that a reader follow those symbolic connections? No, it is quite possible to read the story as a simple adventure tale dealing with two very stubborn men. It is also possible to read "On the Road" as a simple account of what it is to be out of work and hungry, ignoring the broader and deeper implications. But reading sophisticated fiction that way is like reading a plot summary: What you gain is slight compared with what you miss.

HEIGHTENED AWARENESS

Some highly sophisticated works of fiction have almost no figurative language and no symbolic details. Others make extensive use of both. This makes the study of what I have been calling heightened language quite different from such topics as style, plot, or setting. You can't assume that every work of fiction will provide examples.

The first rule for active readers, then, is to stay alert for the possibility of both figurative language and symbolic details. If you read a good deal, you will begin to recognize the cues often provided by writers: the repeated use of a phrase (as in "On the Road"), the special attention given to physical details which do not at first seem essential to the plot (as in "A & P"), and the repetition of certain types of action (as in "Small Point Bridge").

The second rule is to follow up initial hunches. Stop reading for a minute and ask yourself, "Hey, what's going on here?" Consider a hypothesis and then see if you can find a defense for it.

This is not to say that you should always read slowly and deliberately. The pleasure you receive from uninterrupted reading is certainly worth a good deal. So if the work is short, read rapidly and postpone your analysis until you are through. But this becomes increasingly risky with longer and more complex fiction. The best approach with novels is to stop at the end of each chapter and consider whether there are samples of heightened language which you should note before moving on.

TOPICS FOR ANALYSIS

If you are writing a paper, here are three possible approaches you might consider. Because it is important for you to analyze fiction not already discussed here, the questions are more general than some of those at the end of previous chapters. Your specific treatment will depend a great deal on what story or novel you have selected.

1.   Find a short story or a section of a novel which makes use of figurative language. List some of the similes, metaphors, and any samples of hyperbole or personification you find there. Explain them by suggesting how each might be expressed in nonfigurative phrasing. See if you can identify overtones in the figurative language which would be lost in your nonfigurative version.

2.   Select two different works which make use of figurative language. To find the greatest contrast, you might consider fiction written in different centuries. Start by listing the specific examples you want to work with (as suggested in the preceding topic). Then decide what the primary differences are. One work, for example, might use more similes than metaphors. Another might use more elaborate figures of speech than the other.

3.   Analyze one or more symbolic details in a single work. Show how each contributes to the theme. What would be lost if it were eliminated? Try to determine whether the symbolic detail merely adds to what the reader knows from other sources or whether it suggests some new insight.

Even if you do not plan to write a paper on the subject of heightened language, you will find these theme topics useful as a basis for notes on fiction you have been reading. You will be able to respond to the full resonance of a story or novel if you take the time to identify both the figurative language and the symbolic details.

chapter 15

THEMATIC CONCERNS

theme (central concern) defined
multiple themes
layered themes
themes of conviction (theses)
writing about thematic elements
topics for analysis

THEME DEFINED

The *theme* of a novel or story is the abstract suggestion which we draw from the work. Unlike the themes of essays, those in fiction are usually implied rather than directly stated.

The word *theme* has also come to mean a short analytical paper on a specific topic. The only connection is that short essays of this sort should be unified by a single concept, a point to which I will return in the next chapter. What concerns us here is the idea or insight which is the intellectual portion of a work of fiction.

The theme of a story or novel is a very important aspect, but remember that it is only one of many aspects. After all, we don't sit down to read fiction merely to pick out the theme. If we did, we would be implying that fiction is nothing more than a complex and wordy way of presenting philosophical truths. But a sophisticated work of fiction is not an illustrated essay. Rarely is it intended to instruct or persuade like an essay. Instead, fiction creates an illusion of personal experience. We have the sense of making judgments and discoveries on our own, based on what these people do, say, and feel.

For example, instead of being *told* that stubborn and uncompromising men are capable of destroying each other over a minor issue, we observe it happening, take part in the emotional event, and have the illusion of drawing this and other conclusions on our own. Of course, authors do their best to nudge their readers into interpreting a story or novel in a certain way, but the feeling we have as readers is that we are discovering certain patterns and learning about human nature as if we were living through the experience ourselves.

Before we turn to some specific examples, here are three important points which should be kept in mind when examining thematic concerns. First, when we say *theme,* we are usually referring not to a single assertion but to a cluster of related suggestions. For this reason, some critics prefer the phrase *central concern* to *theme.* That reminds us that there are probably several different concerns, one of which is primary. I will use *central concern* interchangeably with *theme* and *thematic concern.*

Closely related to this is the fact that themes are often layered. That is, what seems at first to be *the* theme may have a deeper range of suggestion beneath it. And perhaps one below that as well. When you think you have a clear idea of what the central concern of a story or a novel is, look again. What you first concluded may be accurate but only the top layer.

Finally, themes are rarely didactic—that is, they almost never propose an absolute truth or recommend a particular course of action. They show, reveal, and suggest, but they rarely instruct. There are some interesting exceptions to this which I will examine shortly, but the mainstream of fiction deals with themes, not argumentative theses.

MULTIPLE THEMES

The theme of any sophisticated work of fiction can be described in a number of ways depending on which aspect you wish to emphasize. For example, here is one of several different but valid descriptions of the theme of "Small Point Bridge": When two stubborn and uncompromising men disagree, they may be willing to risk personal disaster in the defense of some small point.

A good short paper could be written supporting this. Isaac's stubbornness is illustrated in the way he battles the winter storms year after year, and Seth's refusal to pay one dollar for twenty years' rent is proof of his own uncompromising nature. One can easily demonstrate how worthless the land is by quoting the descriptions of the island. Then, there is the further evidence of its name, "Small Point," which is highlighted in the title. The fact that both men are willing to risk disaster is supported in that scene on the bridge when they argue with each other even though they may be thrown into the frigid waters at any moment.

But another reader might focus on the forces of nature which are obviously important in that story. He or she might suggest this as the theme: Conflicts between individuals sometimes disappear when they both face a more pressing struggle with nature.

A paper supporting this thematic description would focus first on the opening scene in which we learn about how long Isaac Bates has been battling the winter ice. The storm is almost personified in Isaac's mind when he addresses it directly: "'Snarl all you want . . . . You can't move granite.'" From there the paper might move to the scene on the bridge. When Isaac sees his cannery being "split open like a flowerpot and the records of a lifetime [flying] like snow," he is no longer defiant. In fact, "The brutality of it shocked him. It wasn't like other storms." This is the point when he abandons his campaign to outwit Seth and joins forces with him. In the final scene, the two men are reunited in that little cabin, and the winter ice becomes the common enemy outside.

Which paper would be correct? Which would focus on *the* theme of the story? They would both be valid insights. Each would be developing a different thematic concern. And there are other possibilities as well.

A third writer, for example, might insist that even though the conflict between two willful men is important, and the struggle with nature is a significant part of the story, neither thematic statement places enough emphasis on Isaac himself. He is, this writer might insist, the real core of this story. The descriptions of Seth and those winter storms are merely ways of developing Isaac's personality. This third paper might describe the theme of the story like this: Those who spend most of their lives battling a hostile environment are likely to treat their friends and associates in the same rough and insensitive way.

This paper would, like the first, draw heavily on the opening section, showing how personal the conflict is between Isaac and the winter storms. But unlike the other two papers, it would rely equally on the scene at the end of the story when Isaac is in the cabin with Seth. It is the sight of Seth, sitting there in his foul weather gear, "like something washed up after a storm," that brings Isaac to this moment of self-doubt: "Had he spent a lifetime on that miserable coast only to end up harsh as the sea itself?"

How can three different papers all be essentially "right" in their interpretation of the theme of a story? Because stories like this contain a cluster of closely related themes. These three papers disagree in emphasis, but they do not contradict each other—unless one of them makes the mistake of saying that it represents the only possible interpretation.

This is not to say that a story or novel can mean all things to all people. That statement is the excuse of lazy readers. It is a way of shrugging off the whole notion of theme. Actually, a story contains very specific ideas which are woven together like threads in fabric. In order to identify them, we have to be able to present clear evidence from the story—specific lines of dialogue, action, physical details, and the like. When we describe different themes, we are focusing on different threads, emphasizing different aspects of the story, but they will all be closely interwoven.

This multiplicity of themes becomes compounded in novels. The longer a work is, the wider the scope, and the greater the opportunity to develop a variety of concerns. In fact, if a novel doesn't explore a number of different themes, we may have the feeling that it is "thin" or "obvious." Most novelists, therefore, make full use of the scope of the genre. For this reason it is often risky to sum up *the* theme of a long, complex novel in a single sentence. You run the risk of oversimplifying. In many cases you will be more accurate discussing *a* theme or a *central concern*.

It is usually difficult, if not impossible, to make a final judgment about the theme of a novel while you are reading it. But stay alert to all clues. If you have read previous works by the same author, they may suggest areas to look out for. F. Scott Fitzgerald, for example, both in his novels and a number of his stories, returned to the ways in which wealth and power affect individuals and also how romantic love sustains itself even in a highly sophisticated society. Ernest Hemingway often explored the code of behavior necessary for individuals—usually men—under stress. When reading the novels of Margaret Drabble, pay particular attention to the way in which our society influences and shapes the development of women who are striking out on their own in the 1970s and 1980s.

These are capsule descriptions, of course, and do not apply to all the works of any one author, but they are the type of recurring themes which are worth recalling when you are reading a new novel by an author with whom you are already familiar.

Even if you have not read other works by the same author, keep looking for recurring thematic patterns. The further you move into a work, the greater the opportunity to see similar situations occurring. If you read *A Mother and Two Daughters* by Gail Godwin, for example, you will probably notice while you are in the middle of it that the author is exploring the ways in which a death in the family affects each of these three women. Further, it should become increasingly apparent that you are witnessing three different types of strength: one in the traditional values of the past, one in the willingness to test new lifestyles, and a third in stubborn political and social conscience. These patterns will come to you not because the author has identified them for you but because you begin to understand the three women through what they do, say, and feel.

In order to see those broad, recurring patterns, it is necessary to stop and review a novel every chapter or so. In addition, keep your eye out for those single scenes which may in themselves dramatize an aspect of the theme. The selection quoted from *A Mother and Two Daughters* is a good example. As an independent scene, it is an amusing insight into how aggravating a child can be and also how that very stubbornness can raise in us a little flash of admiration. In the context of the whole novel, however, it also points out how consistent a person's behavior can be even over a period of decades. The willful, obstinate young girl in that passage who has wrecked the day for her parents and yet who somehow wins the admiration of her father is portrayed in the novel as an adult some thirty-seven years later as still willful, still obstinate, still making a mess of her own life and complicating the lives of those around her; and she continues to win the grudging respect of the reader. If you examine that scene carefully when you are reading the novel, you will see how a single scene can present in miniature a theme which is developed much more fully in the novel as a whole.

LAYERED THEMES

One of the pleasures of literary fiction is that we can read it more than once and draw something new from it each time. Sometimes this is because we begin to see other, closely related themes, as just described. Or it may be that the themes are layered and that what we assumed on first reading was *the* theme was in fact only a surface appearance.

John Updike's story "A & P" is a good example of a work with layered themes. The first time through we are tempted to consider the work as a gentle satire of a rather naive young man. The theme, we might conclude, is that when one is young it is easy to fall in love with a perfect stranger and make a fool of yourself in the process.

This is part of the theme, but it is such a small part that one really should take a second look. How can you tell when your analysis is superficial? In this case it helps if you have read other works by the same author. Updike doesn't write such simple and sentimental stories. But let's ignore that kind of evidence. Simply on the basis of the story itself, we should be able to tell that this interpretation of the theme is superficial. The evidence is this: There are just too many important aspects of the story which are not accounted for in our initial description of the theme.

In the previous chapter I explained how the supermarket setting becomes a satiric symbol for the commercial world of shoddy products— American materialism. Understanding this is a first step toward reexamining the theme. As a second step, let's take another look at the narrator who gives us this rather biased description.

Sammy is cheerful, a joker, but he is also capable of taking little things very seriously. His behavior over the three young women who hardly notice him is comic. We smile at him for having some of the intense feelings we associate with adolescence. The author, then, is not only poking fun at supermarkets but at certain kinds of youthful attitudes as well.

What about Lengel, the manager? He is portrayed as one for whom the rules are more important than feelings. "That's policy for you," Sammy comments. "Policy is what the kingpins want. What the others want is juvenile delinquency." Hardly an unbiased description! But it does establish Lengel as being on the opposite side of the fence from Sammy. And both extremes are presented as being just a bit absurd.

Without rejecting our first description of the theme, we can now go a bit deeper. What we want is a statement about the theme which accounts for some of the other elements in the story. Here is a possible description: The absurdity of a romantic and idealistic young man is no less ridiculous than the absurdity of the commercial world and those rigid individuals who take it seriously.

This is a "deeper" analysis because it helps to explain those satiric descriptions of the supermarket and its manager. It also helps us to understand that last scene when Sammy looks back through the window and sees the manager "checking the sheep through" and looking as if he "just had an injection of iron." Sammy has left not only his job but his position in the commercial world, and Lengel has dutifully filled in for him.

Can we go any further? There may come a point, of course, when we begin to read things into the story which aren't really there. But as long as we can support our analysis with specific evidence from the story, we are on safe ground. One detail which remains outside the two thematic descriptions I have proposed so far comes at the very end of the story. The narrator says, "I felt how hard the world was going to be to me hereafter."

Here is a third aspect of the theme, this one reflecting the importance of that ending: The concern for personal values and feelings often runs counter to the demands of the commercial or material aspects of our society. That is, those who act on impulse often have difficulty living in a society which insists on upholding rules and regulations.

Notice the process of analysis. We started with what seemed like a reasonable description of the theme. When we saw that it did not account for some important aspects of the story, we revised it, looking a bit deeper. The third phrasing became more abstract but helped to explain the summary statement at the end of the story. Your analysis will not necessarily develop in layers like this, but it is always worth questioning whatever thematic statement came to mind first.

THEMES OF CONVICTION

I stated earlier that themes in fiction are rarely didactic—that is, they are not intended to teach or instruct. They usually suggest certain concepts or insights rather than state them. There are some exceptions to this, however, and they provide an interesting footnote to literature. They are works in which the subtleties of theme have been replaced by a *thesis*—a proposal or argument for a specific action or type of behavior.

We expect theses in persuasive essays, sermons, political speeches, and the like. But only occasionally do they appear in fictional form. I have already mentioned John Bunyon's *Pilgrim's Progress* in this connection. It is a lesson in how to follow what the author believes to be a Christian life. There is nothing very subtle in this work, but its purpose is primarily to teach. Written as an allegory (see page 109), it is in many ways like an illustrated essay or sermon.

Another example of highly didactic fiction is Harriet Beecher Stowe's *Uncle Tom's Cabin*, which was first published in 1852. Because it is not an allegory, both the characterization and the plot are more realistic than they are in *Pilgrim's Progress;* but they still strike us today as rather wooden. In spite of this, the novel had a significant effect on public attitudes about slavery during the 1850s.

In our own century, novels with strong political and social positions like George Orwell's *Animal Farm* and *1984* influenced public opinion as well. *The Ugly American* by William Lederer and Eugene Burdick is hardly good fiction (it was converted from nonfiction in six days of marathon writing!), but it had a dramatic effect on our State Department in the late 1950s.

Both *utopian* and *antiutopian* novels—those describing an ideal society or one which is terrible—tend to have precise theses rather than themes. Some are really illustrated essays. Didactic novels with blatant theses like these are rare, however. The reason is that what they gain in clarity and impact they lose in subtlety and credibility. (The same applies to political posters and cartoons as compared with paintings with a strong message, such as the art of Goya and the Mexican painter, Diego Rivera.) In literature, it is characterization which suffers most noticeably when the work becomes didactic. For this reason, it is more common for authors to make their characters credible rather than mere illustrations of a religious or political conviction.

There are many examples of fiction in which intense convictions are muted in order to maintain credibility—particularly of characterization. Charles Dickens, for example, had a strong social conscience and actually had an influence on nineteenth-century reform movements. But he was careful not to preach. His message is made clear and dramatic through the action and the characters. Similarly, the early novels of Graham Greene unmistakably reflect his Catholic faith; but they are not intended to convert the reader. The moral, social, and personal problems faced by Greene's characters are ones which apply in different ways to all people. In the same way, Margaret Drabble, Gail Godwin, and Margaret Atwood are among a large group of authors who are concerned with the status of women in our society, but none of them use fiction to preach.

Of the stories included in this volume, "On the Road" by Langston Hughes is the closest to fiction with a thesis. But even this story does not propose a particular solution. It is charged with deeply felt convictions about our society, but it does not limit its impact by campaigning for a specific bit of legislation. The fact that the story was first published in 1935 and still does not seem "dated" is an indication that it deals with timeless issues.

The theme of this story is also more complex than it could have been in a more didactic work. It is far more than a simple cry for social justice. It speaks for the poor and destitute everywhere, but it also deals with the relationship between blacks and whites in the United States. In addition, it comments on the role of the church in social matters. In Sargeant's dream, Christ walks on earth; in reality, the story suggests, Christ remains on the cross. How are we to include all this in a statement about *the* theme? This is clearly a story in which a number of issues are strongly felt, but the very complexity of these interwoven themes keeps the work on the level of sophisticated fiction.

WRITING ABOUT
THEMATIC ELEMENTS

The approaches I have taken in describing thematic concerns in fiction can be used in the writing of short papers. You may find, for example, that a story or a novel has a group of related themes. If this is the case, pick one out as your primary concern and arrange the others in some kind of logical order. Support each one with specific evidence from the fiction. Refer to scenes and to characters precisely. Use quotations from the fiction when that is appropriate.

Or it may be that you can describe the theme as layered—an initial description followed by more penetrating descriptions of the theme. Once again, you should support your analysis with evidence from the fiction.

If the fiction you are working with reflects the author's strong conviction, look carefully at whether the work presents a precise argument—a true thesis—or whether there are a number of related concerns which, even though strongly felt, are more accurately called themes.

Another possibility is comparing or contrasting the themes of two works. Make sure you understand in advance whether you are going to concentrate on similarities between two themes or some striking contrast. In the case of contrasting themes, there isn't much point in selecting two stories or novels which really have nothing at all in common. It is far more effective to look for works which are in the same area yet suggest different concerns or approaches—two novels by and about women, for example; or two stories by black authors. In what ways are the themes of these works similar and how do they differ?

TOPICS FOR ANALYSIS

Here are three questions which could be used as the basis of class discussion or as theme topics. Although the first one springs from analysis touched on in this chapter, it will require fresh and original thought. The other two should be adapted to works not included here.

     1.   Examine the thematic concerns in "On the Road." Is this story best described as having a central and dominant theme with a cluster of related concerns? Or is it more accurate to describe the theme as layered? In your analysis, define exactly what you feel these various concerns are, and show how the author reveals them through action, dialogue, and description.

     2.   Select a story or novel with a central concern which is fairly easy to define. Read the work a second time and then describe how you in your own first reading came to understand that theme. That is, see if you can reconstruct the stages by which you discovered what the major theme was. Concentrate on the process by which you put those pieces together, picking out specific details which gave you that understanding.

     3.   Select two works which have somewhat similar themes. Compare them, showing in what ways they agree. Then contrast both their particular views and the techniques by which they develop their themes.

The theme of a story or novel is only one part of that work. As you study the theme, be careful not to lose track of other aspects such as style, characterization, setting, and the like. But you can be sure that you are moving into the heart of a work of fiction when you carefully examine the thematic concerns.

chapter 16

WRITING ABOUT FICTION

the value of writing papers
topics and thesis statements
outlines
card file for sources
writing the first draft
rewriting and proofreading
reviewing your work after it is
graded

THE VALUE
OF WRITING PAPERS

Writing a paper is one of the best methods you have to examine a literary work in depth. Although reading someone else's analysis can help you to discover what to look for, your involvement with the literary work itself remains relatively passive. When you write an analytical paper, however, what we have been calling active reading is intensified. You become a literary detective, examining evidence, testing theories, coming to conclusions of your own. When you are finished, you not only have produced a paper, you have acquired a personal understanding of a work of fiction which is probably broader and deeper than the thesis you set out to prove.

In addition to learning a great deal about a particular work, you are teaching yourself how to draw the most from literature in general. The process of writing a paper necessarily involves a number of different activities: reading intensively, analyzing, forming your own opinion, finding evidence to support your views, and organizing your ideas. Every paper you write improves your ability to analyze and enjoy whatever else you read. This skill becomes internalized and will remain with you for the rest of your life.

Try to keep these benefits in mind as you face a new assignment. If you start thinking of it as merely a task to be completed for a grade, that may be what it will become. But if you can see the act of writing a paper as a learning process, you will benefit from every stage of the process.

This positive approach will help you with all kinds of writing—the two-page mini-theme, the four-page weekly paper, the term paper, and even the theses required for advanced degrees. Don't be put off by the fact that what you write as a student may have been done by others; don't downplay your own work because it is probably not publishable; and don't for a minute think that because your paper is short it is of no value. Its true worth is what it does for your own development. You are discovering aspects of a particular literary work on your own, and at the same time you are training yourself to read in depth. On a still broader level, you are developing your ability to think and write clearly.

TOPICS AND THESIS STATEMENTS

A *topic* is a general subject for analysis. "A contrast between two different literary styles" is a topic. "Some differences between the style of Joseph Conrad and Ernest Hemingway" is a more specific topic.

A *thesis* is an assertion. When you state a thesis, you are usually taking a position. Here, for example, is a thesis statement based on the same topic: "The style of Joseph Conrad tends to be characterized by longer, more complex sentences than that of Ernest Hemingway." Here is a slightly more detailed version of that: "The style of Joseph Conrad can be distinguished from that of Ernest Hemingway by differences in diction, syntax, and use of figurative language."

As you can see from these examples, a thesis statement is usually more specific than a topic. More important, a thesis statement is normally described in a complete sentence. This is a significant difference because only when you use a full sentence with a subject and a verb do you have an assertion which can be defended.

Theme assignments tend to fall into three categories, and each requires a somewhat different approach. Some are "free" or "open," leaving even the topic up to you. More often, they propose a topic, allowing you to find your own thesis. Occasionally they may provide the thesis itself, leaving to you the task of gathering the evidence and presenting the material in the most logical and persuasive manner. Essay questions in examinations often take this third form. Try to keep these distinctions in mind as you look over a theme assignment or examination question. Judge carefully just what is required.

"Free" or "open" assignments bother some students because they seem to offer too many choices. There is an advantage in this approach, however, in that it allows you to select a subject which really interests you. One way to get started on an analytical paper is to apply the topics which precede each chapter in this book (specific headings are listed in the Table of Contents) to a story or novel which you have already read. For example, if characterization interests you, the headings for Chapter 3 suggest that you consider the differences between flat and round characters, the ways character is revealed through the five narrative modes, and so on. Or if tension seems to be a likely subject, the headings for Chapter 9 suggest that you examine the ways your author has established conflict, suspense, or moments of surprise. In addition to proposing possible topics for papers, these headings also serve as a quick review of literary concerns.

When the assignment provides you with a topic, your next step is to devise a thesis statement which will serve as the core of your paper. In fact, even if the assignment looks like a fairly manageable thesis, consider narrowing the field and making it even more specific. This is particularly important if the paper is to be a short one. There is a very common tendency to take on too broad a concern for the length of the paper, so make a special effort to limit the scope of your thesis.

Suppose, for example, the assigned topic is "Compare the characterization of Sargeant in 'On the Road' with that of Sammy in 'A & P.'" This is a topic, not a thesis statement. True, it is presented in the form of a complete sentence, but it is not yet an assertion. It is up to you to make a statement about the characterization of these two protagonists and to support it with evidence from each story.

After reading over both stories, you might decide on something like this: "The character of Sargeant is presented primarily through action, while Sammy's is revealed mainly through his own words." You would want to qualify this in the body of the paper since Sammy does perform one significant act: He takes a stand and loses his job. Still, the thesis can be defended by describing those dramatic scenes in "On the Road" and comparing that pattern with the revealing monologue in "A & P."

If you wanted a thesis with a slightly different emphasis, you might take this approach: "Characterization in 'On the Road' is essentially a social statement, while that in 'A & P' is more precisely the study of an individual." In this paper, you would want to show how Sargeant is to some degree a composite description of a segment of our society. The story is not just about an individual; it is a statement about all of those who are poor and black. The characterization in "A & P," on the other hand, focuses more directly on a single individual and only very indirectly touches on social issues.

When a suggested topic deals with novels, the need for limiting your thesis to a manageable size is even more important. Suppose, for example, you are asked to write a short paper contrasting the use of setting in two different novels. You may want to make an assertion about the general difference (one work may use setting in a symbolic way, for example, and the other merely as background), but then focus on specific scenes. If your assignment calls for a three-page paper, you may have to limit yourself to one scene from each work, suggesting that these represent a more general pattern. With a longer paper, you could use two or three different examples. In either case, make sure that you support your thesis with specific evidence from each novel.

Here are two topics, each followed by two possible theses. I have not used actual titles or authors because my concern is for the general technique of finding thesis statements which you can apply to the fiction you have been reading. Remember that the shorter the paper the more specific and restricted the thesis should be.

> *Topic:* "Contrast two uses of dramatic conflict."
>
> *A thesis statement:* "In novel *A* the primary conflict, a sustained struggle between an individual and society, is stronger but less subtle than the conflict in novel *B*, a series of misunderstandings between husband and wife as well as between parents and children."

This is a fairly elaborate thesis because there are several aspects, each of which should be supported with evidence. It would probably be more appropriate for a substantial paper than it would be for a brief weekly theme. If you wanted to reduce the scope, you might consider something like this: "The climax at the end of novel *A* is more dramatic but less subtle than the concluding scene of novel *B*." In many cases you can narrow the field of a thesis by concentrating in this way on one aspect or on specific scenes.

> *Topic:* "Analyze the differences between flat and round characters in story *A* or story *B*."
>
> *A thesis statement:* "The protagonist and his son in story *B* are the only fully drawn or round characters, but there are three flat characters who are essential to the plot."

This thesis requires examining a total of five characters. If your paper is to be relatively short, it might be wise to try something more limited, like this: "The protagonist in story *A* is fully drawn and provides a sharp contrast with her brother, who remains a flat character throughout the story."

Notice, incidentally, that the original topic called for an analysis of characters in *either* story, not both. It is very important to look at the wording carefully—especially in essay-type examination questions where time is an important factor.

Whenever possible, decide on a thesis statement before you write your first draft. You may have to spend some time testing different possibilities, but having a thesis as your base will help to keep you on course and will often save you a lot of rewriting later.

There are occasions, however, when a clear thesis just doesn't come to mind. Everyone has had the experience of staring at a blank piece of paper with no notion of where to start. In such cases, try rereading the fiction and then "free writing"—informally recording some thoughts about the story or novel as if you were writing a journal entry. Postpone decisions about the organization, but try to stay on the general subject. Often the very act of placing some random observations on paper will break your "writer's block" and get you going. Remember, though, that what you are writing is merely for your own use. It is the raw material from which an organized paper can be drawn.

OUTLINES

Once your ideas begin to take shape, you may be tempted to start your first draft at once. Many students and professional writers as well, however, find it extremely helpful to write an outline first. Although it may seem to take valuable time, there are a number of advantages which are well worth considering. First, preparing an outline before writing the first draft often saves time in the long run. This is because you tend to do much less radical revision of the first draft if you have moved logically from point to point the first time through. Second, outlining is a safeguard against writing a paper which begins to make one assertion and ends up making another. The organizational structure and logical sequence are easier to see in outline form than in a completed draft. Third, outlines provide an effective way to judge whether you have supported your analysis with sufficient evidence from the story or novel. They can also be used as a handy record of where your references came from. Above all, outlines are your best safeguard against producing a paper which ends up being merely a plot summary.

You should not, of course, be slavish to your outline. Revisions in emphasis or even structure may occur to you as you write the paper. Having an outline, however, is like plotting a course: Even when you revise it, you will have a clear notion of what direction you are taking.

A basic, adaptable form of outline uses major headings and only one set of subheadings. These headings are usually written as phrases, not complete sentences, and they are not punctuated. Since the outline is for your own use, any abbreviations which make sense to you are useful. It is usually wise to write out your thesis statement at the top of the page as a reminder. Here is a sample outline of a short theme based on the selections by Gwendolyn Brooks and Gail Godwin reprinted in Chapter 10.

THESIS: The excerpts by Gwendolyn Brooks and Gail Godwin illustrate the difference between suspense and dramatic conflict.

   I.   Intro: Thesis statement (above)
       A. suspense defined
       B. dramatic conflict defined
  II. Tension as seen in the Brooks excerpt
       A. impact of withheld information
       B. different reactions by members of family
       C. joyful resolution shared by reader
 III. Conflict as seen in the Godwin excerpt
       A. basic struggle between grandfather & granddaughter
       B. parents (& reader) caught between
       C. resolution leaves all characters dissatisfied
       D. ambivalence about daughter shared by reader
 IV. Basic contrasts in tension
       A. suspense can be created w/out combatants
       B. conflict usually based on two opposed forces

This is a basic, practical type of outline. No frills. If you use this form at least once as a model, you will discover how it helps the writing process. After that, you may want to vary the pattern to suit your own needs and inclinations.

How many headings should you use? That depends mainly on how long the paper will be. If you are doing a three-page theme, two or three major headings with just one set of lettered subheadings (such as I used in the preceding outline) will almost always be enough. This is called a "two-tier outline." A term paper, on the other hand, may have as many as six or seven major headings. It is generally a good idea, however, to consolidate your main headings so you can keep the organizational structure clearly in mind while writing.

If you add a third tier of subheadings, use Arabic numerals: 1, 2, 3, and so on. A fourth tier can be identified with lower-case letters: a, b, c, and so forth. Notice that each set of headings switches back and forth from numerals to letters just for the sake of clarity. Here is the beginning of a four-tier outline based on what might be a longer paper on the novels from which the two excerpts were taken.

THESIS: The plots in *Maud Martha* and in *A Mother and Two Daughters* illustrate the difference between single and multitrack structure.

   I.   Structure of *Maud Martha* focuses on protagonist
       A. chronology follows her life
          1. childhood experiences
             a. financial insecurity
             b. strong family bonds
             c. sense of values established
          2. young woman

    3. married life
        a. high hopes not realized
        b. inner strengths shown
    B. scenes unrelated except through characterization
II. Structure of *A Mother* . . . based on 3 char. equally
    A. opening chapters focus on mother

In addition to organizing your paper, outlines also serve as a useful record of your research sources. Even short themes usually need quotations and direct references to the literary work being analyzed. In longer papers you may be quoting secondary sources as well. It is all too easy to lose track of where these came from. The simplest way to keep an informal record of each is to note the title and page number in parentheses in your outline.

If you have many quotations and references, you may want to consider using a card-file approach. Buy a pack of standard 3 × 5 file cards (or the larger 5 × 8 size) and write each quotation and specific reference on a separate card. In the upper left corner, describe what aspect of your topic this concerns, and in the upper right record the book and page. Use your own abbreviations to save writing out the author and title each time.

If you number each card, you can enter that number in your outline. This saves more time. Remember that the whole system should be modified by your own preferences and by the demands of the research project.

One variation, for example, is to write the entire outline on a series of cards. The advantage of this approach is that you can rearrange the organization without having to copy over the outline. The disadvantage is not being able to see the entire structure displayed on a single page.

Whatever system you use, make sure that your paper does not degenerate into a mere summary of the action. To guard against that, keep your thesis statement clearly in mind. Every paragraph should contribute directly to developing that basic assertion.

In addition, pay special attention to the order in which you present your material—both the major headings and your minor ones. Try to provide some reason for the sequence you have selected. In some cases you might move chronologically, following the order in the story or novel itself. In other cases you will want to move from the most important point to the least—or the reverse. Another pattern which lends itself to papers comparing two works is alternation—first one story, for example, and then the other. Both of the sample outlines given earlier use this method of alternating two works, but the second describes the divisions of the first novel chronologically. Having some kind of system helps the reader see why your material is arranged as it is. This is the first step toward establishing what is known as *coherence*.

Every writer has a different attitude toward outlining. And every project has a different set of demands. If you try various approaches, you will soon find how helpful outlining can be and also which type is right for you.

THE FIRST DRAFT

If you have a clear, logical outline, the writing of your first draft may be smooth and relatively effortless. Sometimes it takes even less time than it did to organize your ideas and find evidence to support them. In such happy cases, follow your outline closely.

Occasionally, however, you will want to make revisions as you write. A shift in order may occur to you. Or one point may be naturally broken into two. If there is a specific requirement about length, you may find that the first draft is beginning to go over the limit or threatens to fall short of the minimum. If you decide on a radical shift in approach, it is often wise to work out a revised outline so you can keep track of what you are doing.

As you write, keep referring to your outline. Translate the headings you have there into paragraph topics. In many cases the wording of those headings will quite naturally become the *topic sentence* of a paragraph—a sentence which announces the central concern of the paragraph which follows.

Suppose, for example, you are writing a short paper on Carson McCullers' "The Sojourner" and have settled on this is a working thesis: "Symbolic details in 'The Sojourner' which have to do with mortality and rootlessness are contrasted with those depicting a happy family unit." The major headings for such a paper might be as follows:

    I.   Symbolic details suggesting age and death
   II.   Details suggesting rootlessness
 III.   Details suggesting family stability

Your first paragraph might well be a brief one introducing your thesis as a whole. Here is one possible opening sentence:

> Although there are many symbolic details in Carson McCullers' "The Sojourner," they generally fall into three categories: Those which suggest age and death, those which give the feeling of rootless wandering, and, in contrast, those which give us pictures of family unity and stability.

In this case, the working thesis has been expanded to form the introductory sentence without much change. In other cases, the conversion may be more complicated. But the same general approach can be used with the paragraphs which follow. The second paragraph would be based on the first major heading and might begin like this:

The first symbolic suggestion of mortality and death appears in the third paragraph of the story: "Ferris had come from Paris to his father's funeral . . . ." Although this does not appear significant at the time, we later see it as a recurring reference.

Both this and the proposed opening for the first paragraph are topic sentences. Each announces the subject of the paragraph as a whole. Topic sentences can also be placed at the end of a paragraph or somewhere in the middle. Or they can be merely implied rather than stated. But there are two advantages to beginning a paragraph with a topic sentence, especially in academic papers. First, it clarifies your intent for the reader. In addition, if you are writing an in-class theme or an essay question in an examination, using a topic sentence helps you to keep the paragraph unified.

Returning to the theme, we are now about to begin the third paragraph. Refer once again to the outline and expand your second major heading:

The sensation of rootlessness and wandering is suggested at the very outset on the story. As he wakes, his thoughts turn to a succession of foreign scenes . . . .

After you complete a description of those symbolic details, your next paragraph will develop naturally from your third major heading:

These symbolic suggestions provide a sharp contrast with those portraying the stability and permanence of a harmonious family unit.

A final paragraph could be devoted to a summary or conclusion. This is particularly helpful if the subject matter in the paper is fairly complex. If the paper is brief, however, and the thesis entirely clear, it can be implied rather than stated.

If the paper is to be six or eight pages rather than two or three, some of these major headings should be divided into separate paragraphs. In most cases, the subheadings will serve as the basis of paragraphs just as the major headings did in the shorter paper.

REWRITING
AND PROOFREADING

How much should you revise the first draft? It all depends on how complete your outline is and on how successfully it served as a guide. Do keep in mind, however, that writing is usually a messy, complex activity, requiring reexamination at every stage. Even professionals often spend more time tinkering with a first draft than they do on the original writing.

If your first draft was written without any outline, it may be worth writing one out at this stage. If you have trouble figuring out just what the logical sequence of the paper is, this may be an indication that the paper itself needs some basic revisions.

Even if you prepared an outline which was complete and helpful, there may be revisions and corrections which will occur to you only after the first draft is complete. As you look over your work, start examining the largest concerns first: organization, logical structure, coherence, and the like. When you are satisfied with that, examine individual paragraphs and finally smaller units like sentence structure and diction. There is no rigid formula for this, but here is a general pattern for examining your own first-draft work:

1.   *Overview:* Have you followed your original plan? Or if not, has the revised organization held together logically? Read over your thesis statement (once again) and compare it with your opening paragraph and your closing paragraph. Did you end up where you said you would?

It is not at all unusual to have a first draft announce one thematic intent in the beginning and end up suggesting something quite different. In some cases this will show you what your real thesis is. You will have to decide which approach is the most insightful and revise accordingly.

Also examine the order of the paragraphs. What appeared logical in the outline may seem less justified in the rough draft. In the example I proposed, for example, the second major heading (II) refers to the scene which appears first in the story. This may be a good reason for revising the order of the major headings, placing the second one first. Or was the order based on how significant or how important each was? These are questions which really should be asked when you are working out your outline, but sometimes they do not occur to you until you see a rough draft on the page.

2.   *Paragraphs:* Are they unified? Not all your paragraphs will have a clearly stated topic sentence, but each should have a central concern. Read over the first sentence of each paragraph. In many cases it will be a topic sentence even without your planning it that way. But if it is not, make sure that what follows is a logical unit.

Also check the transitions or linkages which connect these paragraphs. Transitions are formed with phrases like these: "The most obvious characteristic of her style is . . . ." "A third use of symbolic language is found in . . . ." "On the other hand," "The final and most dramatic use of setting is seen in . . . ." These are the signposts your reader needs to indicate why you have arranged the material the way you did and where the paper is going.

3.   *Sentences:* Are they complete? If you are secretly unsure of what makes a sentence incomplete or where to put commas, you really should consider one of these two alternatives: First, you can study a grammar book. You will find that the system is really simpler than you imagined. A half hour of study each afternoon for two weeks will save you a lifetime of uncertainty and embarrassment. Or you can turn to a writing clinic or remedial class. These are not designed to punish; they are

offered to help you. If you enter with this in mind, you can learn a lot in a short time.

In addition to grammatical correctness (note the transitional phrase), there is the matter of giving pleasure to the reader (topic sentence). Are some sentences short? Sentence variation does a lot to keep prose from becoming dull. Are some too long? Above all (a highlighting phrase), delete any sentence which is a truism—a statement or phrase which is too obvious to be placed in print. For example: "Shakespeare was a masterful dramatist"; "Novels tend to be longer than stories"; "Literature has been around for a long time." Such sentences are empty baggage, but they do show up—especially when you are trying to pad a paper to make it longer. The best way to expand a paper is to strike out the say-nothing sentence and add a whole new paragraph which really contributes to your basic thesis.

4. *Phrases:* Watch out for *clichés* and *hackneyed language.* Clichés are usually conventional similes or metaphors which have been used so frequently they tend to deaden rather than enliven your style: "to toe the line," for example, or "crystal clear." Hackneyed language is a broader category which includes any phrase which has been overused. Many of them are alliterative (matching initial sounds) and redundant, like "each and every," "tried and true," and "last but not least." Others are just plain corny. Referring to Shakespeare as "the Bard," to Wordsworth as "that immortal poet," or to a fictional scene as creating "magic" all tend to add a musty, dated tone to your style. If in doubt, say it straight.

5. *Words:* Make sure you are using them correctly. Watch out for those rare and fancy ones which show up in vocabulary-building lists. There is nothing wrong with expanding your vocabulary in this manner, but make sure that you have seen a word on several occasions before you begin to use it yourself.

Incidentally, one of the best ways to increase your vocabulary is to read regularly and look up the words you don't understand. Keep a record of them and quiz yourself at least once a week.

In addition to correctness, try to achieve vitality in your word choice. Keep adjectives and adverbs to a minimum. You won't need more than a few if you find the most effective nouns and verbs. Strike out all lazy modifiers like "very" and "sort of," and avoid vague nouns like "thing." For example, cross out a sentence like "The best thing about this very well-written story is how it sort of holds your attention." Replace it with something like this: "The appeal of this story is its ability to grip your attention." Using the right nouns and effective verbs will give your writing impact.

Next, there is the matter of spelling. Is it important? It sure is. Misspelled words detract not only from academic papers, but from all types of writing from job applications to committee reports and legal briefs.

If you are a poor speller, there are positive steps you can take. Although there are no quick cures, it helps to record your errors regularly, study them, and look for patterns. In addition, there is one technique which has helped thousands of students. It requires fifteen minutes a day for three months.

Keep track of your errors and record the correct spelling on 3 × 5 cards—just three to a card. Have someone quiz you (or quiz yourself on a cassette recorder) every morning. If you work with three cards you will have nine words and the daily quiz will take less than five minutes. Place a check after each word you spell correctly. Study them all for ten minutes. Repeat the process the next day. Do not throw a card away until you have three checks after each of the three words. Every time you discard a card, replace it with another. Work regularly, six days a week for three months. The system is astonishingly effective.

6. *The manuscript:* Proofread your final copy and make sure that it is as free from errors as possible. There is no such thing as a "good paper with bad mechanics." That's like saying, "It's a good meal but badly cooked."

Marshall McLuhan coined what has now become a too-familiar slogan: "The medium is the message." That may be overstating the case, but it is a dramatic reminder of the fact that the medium—your manuscript—is a significant part of the statement you are making. If your typing is sloppy and there are words crossed out or corrected in ink, you are saying, "I don't take this subject very seriously." A carefully prepared paper, on the other hand, announces to the reader that you consider your work important and you expect it to be read with care.

AFTER THE GRADE

An academic paper is usually given a grade. Everyone pretends that grades are meaningless and evil (a "necessary evil" is the hackneyed phrase most often used). But actually grades have both a meaning and a virtue: They define fairly precisely what your critic thinks of your work. (Students in schools which do not grade often complain that they do not know how well they are doing.) As for the virtue, grades stimulate an enormous amount of effort—both by you in the writing and by your teachers in the evaluating.

But don't let your completed paper become "just a grade." If the writing of the paper was an important learning experience, a review of the result is a continuation of that process. Read carefully whatever comment you receive. Make sure you really understand what could have been improved. If the comment is detailed, jot down the main points in your notebook so that you can compare it with others made during the term.

If the written comments are brief or you can't read the handwriting, ask for a conference. Don't turn your meeting into a bargaining session over grades. Unless there has been some kind of mathematical error, complaints like that tend to make the session negative and unproductive. Instead, think of the conference as a mutual exploration of exactly what worked and what could be improved. You can help to establish that tone if you come to the conference with some specific questions. As the discussion develops, take a few notes. You may find them helpful when you begin your next paper.

One final point on the writing of academic papers: You will forget the specifics of the paper—including the grade—in a month, and a good deal of the course in five years. But your ability to read fiction in greater depth and really enjoy it will stay with you for the rest of your life.

chapter 17

ENJOYING FICTION

OBSTACLES FOR READERS

The focus of this book has been on how to draw the most from the fiction you read. But I am also concerned with the pleasure of reading. The two goals are actually a part of the same process since a greater awareness of what fiction has to offer tends to increase your personal satisfaction.

With this in mind, the real test of a course in the reading of fiction—and of any book like this one—comes after you have finished the last exam: Do you read more and derive more pleasure from your reading?

Most students finish a course in fiction with a determination to read more—not because they *should* but simply because they want to. After all, if you increase any skill such as the ability to play a musical instrument or a sport, there is often a desire to continue on your own if you can. There are, however, certain obstacles to regular reading of fiction which may appear to be worse than they really are.

One apparent problem is that books—especially hard-cover novels—seem to cost far too much. But when you look at the price, consider this: No matter what the inflation rate, a novel even in hardback costs less than a rock concert or dinner for two at a good restaurant. And while both of these activities have their place, a novel is still with you the next day. It is something you can enjoy over a period of time and lend to a friend, sharing the experience.

For those on budgets really too tight for concerts *or* novels, there are libraries. They are free and have a great deal to offer.

Another apparent problem is finding time. It is true that many people—especially students who are also holding jobs—have very few free hours. Adding a "spare-time" activity may seem just about impossible. Yet if you have a book which you enjoy, it is surprising how frequently you will pick it up. Even if you are unable to devote solid blocks of time to it, you may find that having something which you are not obliged to do is a welcome relief to an otherwise tight schedule. The only way you can test whether this would apply to you is to have an enjoyable novel or collection of stories handy.

There is a third problem which is a bit more complicated. Sometimes it seems difficult to find the kind of fiction you really enjoy. The situation does not stem from any lack of good novels and short stories. As much, if not more, good fiction is being published today as in any period in our history. But all those titles are shelved alphabetically in bookstores and it is difficult indeed to judge a book by its dust-jacket description.

The problem is increased by the fact that fiction is no longer dominated by a small group of major novelists. When we think of the 1920s and 1930s, a list of prolific authors come to mind: Joyce, Hemingway, Faulkner, Fitzgerald, Steinbeck. The literary scene today is more diffuse—spread over a wide range of styles, concerns, and subject matter. It is no wonder that some readers have turned to book clubs and best-seller lists to make their choices.

But you are the best judge of which novels and short stories are going to give you the most satisfaction. This chapter is intended to help you find what is available and to choose those which meet your particular interests.

FINDING GOOD
SHORT STORIES

There are not as many large-circulation magazines publishing short stories today as there were twenty years ago, but the loss is not as bad as it may seem. Many of the magazines which failed were publishing formula fiction—not significantly different from the daytime television dramas which replaced them.

There are still three large-circulation magazines which publish fiction regularly. I would recommend subscribing to at least one. (Teachers and full-time students can subscribe at substantial savings through the Educational Subscription Service, South Point Plaza, Lansing, MI 48910.) You are far more likely to read the magazine regularly if it is delivered, and even the regular subscription rate is usually half the price of individual copies.

- *The New Yorker* has been publishing two stories almost every week—nearly a hundred a year—for decades. One story is usually light and satiric while the other is often a work of real substance. Contrary to its reputation, the magazine does not specialize in any one style. Some stories are traditional in method, others are highly innovative. *The New Yorker*'s commitment to good fiction is the strongest of any major-circulation magazine now publishing. Don't be put off by the opulent ads.
- *The Atlantic Monthly* publishes one or occasionally two stories in each issue. In addition to work by established authors, the magazine also prints stories by previously unpublished writers. These "Atlantic First" stories add variety and freshness to their offerings.
- *Esquire* publishes fortnightly and usually has one story in each issue.

In addition to the large-circulation magazines, there are over a hundred "little magazines" publishing in this country. They are usually "little" both in format and in circulation, but not in importance to the literary community. They publish the bulk of new short fiction—both innovative and traditional.

In spite of their value, they are difficult to find. If you do not live in a major city or attend a university with an enlightened bookstore, you will have to turn to your college or community library. Find out what little magazines they have. They will be in the periodicals section, usually in open racks along with many nonliterary publications. Some libraries have a special list under the heading of "literary magazines" or "quarterlies" (a policy which should be encouraged). But if they do not, you may wish to use the following brief, alphabetical sampling as an initial guide. Addresses are included here in the event that you are not near a library and would like to send for a sample copy.

- *Antaeus* (18 W. 30th St., New York, NY 10001): Although published only twice a year, *Antaeus* offers fiction regularly, along with poetry and reviews. Occasional issues are devoted to fiction exclusively.
- *Fiction Network* (P.O. Box 5651, San Francisco, CA 94101): Begun in 1983, this quarterly is one of the few magazines devoted exclusively to fiction.
- *Georgia Review* (University of Georgia, Athens, GA 30602): This quarterly offers fiction, poetry, and reviews. Like the *Missouri Review*, it offers special awards for fiction.
- *Mississippi Review* (University of Southern Mississippi, Southern Station, Box 5144, Hattiesburg, MS 39406): Edited by Frederick Barthelme, *MR* is in no way limited to a regional scene. It publishes a wide range of fiction from traditional to innovative. It is published three times a year.
- *The Missouri Review* (231 Arts & Science, University of Missouri, Columbia, MO 65211): This is a quarterly with a good representation of fiction.
- *The North American Review* (University of Northern Iowa, Cedar Falls, IA 50614): The oldest quarterly in the United States, *NAR* maintains a particularly

strong commitment to new fiction. In 1981 and again in 1983 it received the National Magazine Award for Fiction (with *The New Yorker, Esquire,* and *The Atlantic* as runners-up!).

• *Ploughshares* (Box 529, Cambridge, MA 02139). Relatively new, this quarterly rotates its editorship for variety. Special issues are occasionally devoted to poetry, but most contain several stories. Their all-fiction issues are excellent and, when available, serve well as inexpensive anthologies of contemporary fiction.

This is only a brief sampling of the hundred or so small-circulation magazines publishing in this country. Those listed here emphasize fiction, but many others regularly run one or two stories in every issue. Your library should subscribe to all of these. If it does not, you might suggest that it add the missing ones to its list.

The best procedure to follow is to read a few copies of a number of different magazines. Select the one you enjoy the most and send for a year's subscription. The cost will be less than a single meal in a restaurant, and the satisfaction will be prolonged over a year. I stress subscribing because magazines of this sort are not easily digested in a single sitting in a library. You will enjoy each story more if you can read it at your leisure. Keep these magazines for reference. If you maintain a record of which stories were particularly good, you will find yourself returning to them years from now.

You can double your pleasure if you and a friend each subscribe to a different periodical. By trading copies, you will have twice as much reading for the price, and you will also enjoy discussing the fiction you have shared.

In addition to magazines, there are annual collections of short stories which can give you a fine overview of good, contemporary fiction. Many such collections can be found in libraries, but once again I would recommend buying at least one a year.

• *The Best American Short Stories* (Houghton Mifflin Co.): Edited for thirty-six years by Martha Foley, this collection is still referred to informally as "the Foley collection." The editorship is now changed each year.

• *Prize Stories, the O. Henry Awards* (William Abrahams, ed., Doubleday & Co.): Better known as "the O. Henry collection," this is another view of the best fiction published during the previous year.

• *Pushcart Prize, Best of the Small Presses* (Pushcart Press): This annual collection contains poetry and essays as well as fiction, but it is well worth owning for the fiction alone. Most of the selections were originally nominated by editors of little magazines and perhaps for this reason tend to be more innovative than those in the two previously mentioned collections.

• *Illinois Short Fiction Series* (University of Illinois Press, Urbana, IL 61801): The University of Illinois Press has been publishing four paperback collections of stories each year since 1975. Each volume is devoted to the work of a single author. If you write to the press, they will send you a list of titles available.

This admirable policy has more recently been adopted in modified form by the Johns Hopkins University Press (Baltimore, MD 21218), by the University of Pittsburgh Press (Pittsburgh, PA 15260), and by a few others.

FINDING GOOD NOVELS

"I just can't find good novels to read." This is a very common complaint. But as I have pointed out, the problem is with the search, not the supply. There are many titles from which to choose, but it does require a little effort to find what meets your particular interests. Here are four simple ways of going about it:

Select by Author

If you have read something you have enjoyed, see what else is available by that same writer. Most bookstores arrange their fiction sections alphabetically by author, and it is far more fruitful to look for the name of a particular novelist than to browse.

Or you may wish to use the library. Find out what the library has by looking up the authors you have enjoyed. I stress buying because it is a pleasure to be able to mark in your own book, to keep it for as long as you like, and to lend it to friends. But the library is also an excellent source and may well have a better selection than a local bookstore.

Where should you start? Begin by making a list of those authors you enjoyed in school or college. Don't limit yourself to twentieth-century writers. Remember that the eighteenth and nineteenth centuries offer you astonishing variety.

Then review the authors whose works are included in this volume. Here is a complete list with the title of the volume from which each selection was taken:

> Carson McCullers: "The Sojourner" appears in *The Ballad of the Sad Cafe and Collected Short Stories*, published by Houghton Mifflin Co.
>
> Langston Hughes: "On the Road" appears in *Laughing to Keep from Crying*, published by Henry Holt & Co., Inc.
>
> John Updike: "A & P" appears in *Pigeon Feathers and Other Stories*, published by Alfred A. Knopf, Inc.
>
> Stephen Minot: "Small Point Bridge" appears in *Crossings, Stories by Stephen Minot*, published by the University of Illinois Press.
>
> Gwendolyn Brooks: The excerpt is from her novel entitled *Maud Martha*, published by Harper & Bros.
>
> Gail Godwin: The excerpt is from *A Mother and Two Daughters*, published by The Viking Press (also available in paperback).
>
> Joseph Conrad: The excerpt is from *Youth*, a short novel available in a variety of paperback editions.
>
> Ernest Hemingway: The excerpt is from *The Sun Also Rises*, published by Charles Scribner's Sons.

As you read, you will begin to acquire a longer list of authors whose work you frequently enjoy. This shouldn't be your only method of deciding what to read, but it is a good first step.

Read Reviews

If you live in a major city, your local newspaper may have a book-review section in the Sunday edition. Such sections usually review one or two novels a week. You can often tell from the description whether it is a work which you might enjoy—even if the reviewer does not.

The New York Times Book Review is widely read, though often it includes no more than four serious novels in any one issue. Works by established authors are also reviewed in *Newsweek* and *Time*. For a more scholarly approach, try the *New York Review of Books*. To see what is going on with the smaller presses and publishing collectives, consult these two good sources: *The American Book Review* (P.O. Box 188, Cooper Station, New York, NY 10003) and the *San Francisco Review of Books* (1111 Kearny St., San Francisco, CA 94133).

Remember, too, that many little magazines like *The Sewanee Review, The Virginia Quarterly Review,* and *The Georgia Review* contain excellent book reviews in addition to their offerings in fiction, essays, and poetry. Their analysis of current novels is often more detailed and penetrating than that offered by newspapers.

Consider Book Clubs

Contrary to general belief, the primary advantage of book clubs is not a matter of saving money. Even though the initial lure seems like a bargain, when you have purchased the required number of titles, the per-volume price is about what you would have paid at a discount department store. And your range of choice (limited largely to "best sellers") will have been about the same. Remember too that most general book clubs stress nonfiction. Less than a third of their offerings are fiction. Of those, a good proportion are what is known in the trade as "manufactured fiction," commercial products produced for a mass market.

In all fairness, however, I should mention one distinct advantage of book clubs—and one which is not stressed in their advertising. Books do come into your home. Often it will be because you forgot to send the cancel order. You will also find yourself taking a chance on a novel because the bill won't arrive until later. So for those who find it difficult to go into a bookstore and actually pay cash for a novel, book clubs do serve a certain purpose.

Seek the Advice of Friends

This may seem like a superficial approach compared with reading reviews, but in some cases you will learn more from a discussion than you will from a brief review. Naturally, some of your friends will have better advice than others. But seek out those who read fiction and ask them what they recommend. Then buy a copy.

If there is an independent bookstore in your area, include the manager as a valuable resource. Independent bookstores are having great difficulty competing with the increasing number of enormous chain stores (which are run largely by computers). Anyone still willing to stay in business as an independent dealer is probably doing so mainly from a love of books. Such individuals need your business and, in return, can give you valuable advice.

Incidentally, we all share a certain willingness to take a chance when deciding what movie to see or what restaurant to eat at; yet when it comes to buying a novel we sometimes have the feeling that the decision is major one and should be thoroughly researched. We are easily put off by a single bad review or a negative comment from a friend. But it is probably better to take a chance on a new novel or collection of stories than to miss the opportunity of finding a work which you enjoy.

ACQUIRING
THE READING HABIT

There are more than enough habits available which are bad for you. Some make you fat, others can kill you. And most of them will cost you a bundle. An addiction to reading, however, is relatively inexpensive and can only make your life richer.

When you read stories or novels for a course, you are necessarily motivated in part by grades and the hope of credits, in addition to the appeal of the fiction itself. And the choice of what to read is made for you. It is not always an easy transition to shift from that intense and highly directed situation to one in which the choice of what and when to read is entirely yours.

Your first inclination may be to read fairly simple works, ones which don't require much effort. There is nothing wrong with this from time to time. But when you begin to get bored with that kind of writing, remember what you have read for courses and the selections in this book. You now have the ability to read fiction which has a lot to offer.

Try not to think of reading as a moral duty. While it is true that sophisticated fiction expands your mind and broadens your perceptions, thinking about literature that way puts reading on the level of eating balanced meals and brushing your teeth. People read for the same reason they listen to music—for the pleasure of it. Don't deprive yourself. Enjoy.

INDEX-GLOSSARY

This listing may be used both for a quick review of literary terms and as an index. The definitions are limited to the way these terms are applied to fiction. Only the major page references are included. Italicized words indicate cross-references either in the same or a closely related form— for example, metaphorical *refers to* metaphor.

Action, 24. See *narrative modes.*

Active reading, 3ff. A conscious, alert approach to literature, responding to such aspects as the *means of perception, style, theme,* and the like. It is the opposite of "passive reading."

Allegory, 109. A form of extended *metaphor* in which all the *characters* (and often objects and actions as well) in a work of literature are given consistent *metaphorical* meaning. In some cases, this abstract, figurative meaning (see *figure of speech*) is stressed at the expense of credible *characterization.*

Ambivalence, 22. Conflicting emotions which are felt at the same time. Examples: hate and love, fear and attraction.

Antagonist, 69. See *protagonist.*

Antiutopian novel, 122. See *utopian novel.*

As-if-spoken style, 50, 51. Writing which echoes the informal phrasing and word choice we associate with spoken language. Also called "colloquial style."

Authorial voice, 55. Phrases or passages in *fiction* which appear to be from the author's own point of view (see *means of perception*). Frequently such passages are unobtrusive, merely providing factual information which may not be known to the *characters.* In other cases, more common in previous centuries, the author may analyze the characters directly or even speculate on the development of the *plot.*

Autobiography, 48. Writing which is presented (usually in the first *person*) as an accurate, nonfictional account of the author's own life. This is to be distinguished from *fiction* which, though it may be designed to resemble autobiography, is not bound by actual events.

Black humor, 102. See *comedy.*

Central concern, 117. See *theme.*

Character, 18. (1) An individual in fiction (as in "there is only one character in this story"); and (2) the nature or quality of such individuals (as in "her character is fundamentally honest and patient").

Character Change, 22. See *characterization.*

Characterization, 24ff. The portrayal or delineation of a fictional *character.* The techniques used include five *narrative modes* (action, dialogue, thoughts, description, and exposition). The illusion of reality is achieved through the use of consistency, complexity, and individuality. When characters are developed in depth with complexity they are referred to as "round." Such characters often change or develop and so are referred to as "dynamic" as opposed to "static." "Character change" is usually a shift in outlook or attitude rather than an alteration in personality. Characters who are presented only superficially and with a high degree of consistency are called "flat." Since they rarely change in any significant way, they are "static." "Flat" characters who are overly familiar types are "stereotypes" or "stock characters."

Chronological plot, 81. See *plot.*

Cliché, 20. See *hackneyed language.*

Climax, 88. The decisive turning point in a *plot* or, more loosely, the highest point of dramatic impact.

Coherence, 131. Basically, the way a composition hangs together. More technically, it is the logic or other system with which an orderly series of ideas are presented. It applies to elements within a paragraph as well as to the relationship between paragraphs.

Colloquial style, 50. See *as-if-spoken style.*

Comedy, 102. *Fiction* which is light in *tone* and which usually ends happily. Comedy which is gentle and developed through *character* is seen as "humor"; comedy which is clever, biting, and characterized by verbal ingenuity is described as "wit." Macabre, grim, or tragic events treated in a comic fashion are somewhat misleadingly referred to as "black humor."

Complexity, 21. See *characterization.*

Conflict, 68ff. An almost universal form of narrative *tension* which pits *characters* against other characters, a group, a force of nature, or some aspect of themselves. It is also called "dramatic conflict" because of its association with plays.

Connotation, 110. The implications and associations of a word as distinct from its literal or "denotative" meaning. The word "spring," for example, denotes one of the four seasons, but its connotations include rebirth, renewal, youth, and the like. (Also see *symbol.*)

Consistency, 21. See *characterization.*

Cosmic irony, 103. See *irony.*

Costume gothic, 39. See *gothic novel.*

Denotation, 110. See *connotation.*

Description, 26. See *narrative modes.*

Dialogue, 25. See *narrative modes.*

Diction, 97. See *style.*

Dramatic conflict, 68. See *conflict.*

Dramatic question, 69. A brief mystery which arouses the curiosity of readers and holds their attention. Types include questions about whether a *character* will succeed, why a character acted as he or she did, and whether a situation will end in violence. In "suspenseful" novels, dramatic questions are used in quick succession. In simple fiction (see *sophisticated fiction*), the initial dramatic question is often blatant and is called a *hook.*

Dramatic scene,   80. See *scene.*
Dynamic characters,   20. See *characterization.*
Episodic plot,   82. See *plot.*
Exposition,   26. See *narrative modes.*
Factual sequence,   84. See *plot.*
Fiction,   1. An imaginative sequence of events told or written in prose. It is "untrue" in that it comes from the imagination of the author even when it resembles in some respects persons, places, and events in life. Unlike factual writing, fiction is primarily an art form like a musical composition or a painting.
Fictional scene,   80. See *scene.*
Figure of speech,   107. Any word, phrase, or longer passage which departs from its literal meaning to create an implied meaning or special effect. In most cases, the literal meaning is untrue. We respond to the figurative or implied meaning. Similes and *metaphors* are the most common figures of speech. *Irony* is another. Less-used forms include "hyperbole" (exaggeration for effect) and "personification" (investing objects or ideas with human characteristics).
First-person fiction,   48. See *person.*
Flashback,   84. A fictional *scene* which interrupts the continuity of the *plot* by portraying an earlier episode. It is often introduced by a brief use of the past perfect tense ("had . . ."). When many flashbacks are used, it helps to distinguish the "factual sequence" (events as they occurred) from the "narrative sequence" (events as the author has presented them).
Flat characters,   19. See *characterization.*
Frame story,   85. A work of *fiction* which begins with a *narrator* who then either tells a story or introduces another *character* (or characters) who tells a story. Normally, the original narrator concludes the work. In a "front-framed" story or novel the narrator's conclusion is omitted.
Front-framed story,   86. See *frame story.*
Gothic novel,   39. Originally, *fiction* dominated by mystery, horror, and the supernatural. It was called "gothic" because the *setting* was often a gothic castle. "Costume gothic" is a contemporary term which refers to a highly popular form of "simple fiction" (see *sophisticated fiction*) with less emphasis on horror and more on mystery, romance, and elegant period costuming. The castle remains.
Hackneyed language,   135. Overused expressions which have lost all impact because of familiarity. Examples: "last but not least" and "each and every." The "cliché," a special form of hackneyed language, is usually a *metaphor* or simile which has become so familiar from overuse that it no longer has visual impact. "Crystal clear," for example, has less impact than "clear" alone. "Mother nature" is long overdue for retirement and deserves to be replaced by "nature" itself.
Heightened language,   106ff. Language which has been enriched by the use of *figures of speech* (*metaphors*, similes, hyperbole, personification, *irony*), *symbol,* or symbolic overtones. It is common in poetry, frequent in *fiction,* and rare in factual prose.
Historical novel,   39. A novel set in some earlier historical period. Although the term has bad overtones (because of many popular works which are neither historically accurate nor literarily *sophisticated*), some are excellent. For early American history, the works of Kenneth Roberts and Mary Lee Settle provide a high standard.
Hook,   7. A dramatic or mysterious opening scene designed to seize the attention of the reader. It is a relatively obvious type of *dramatic question.*

Humor,   102. See *comedy*.

Hyperbole,   107. See *figure of speech*.

Individuality,   23. See *characterization*.

Irony,   103. A reversal in which the literal statement or actual event is in sharp contrast with the intended meaning or expected outcome. In "verbal irony" the literal statement is different than or even the reverse of the intended meaning. This is similar to sarcasm in speech except that it is not necessarily sneering or caustic in tone. Example: referring to a hurricane as "a great day for a sail." In "cosmic irony" or "irony of fate," the reversal is in events rather than words. Example: A firehouse burns to the ground or an Olympic swimmer drowns in his or her own swimming pool.

Irony of fate,   103. See *irony*.

Layered theme,   120. See *theme*.

Literary fiction,   2. See *sophisticated fiction*.

Means of perception,   6, 52. The agent through whose eyes a *fictional* passage appears to be presented. Synonymous with "point of view." It is frequently limited to a single *character* in short stories ("single" point of view), but in novels it may shift from one character to another ("multiple" point of view). In addition, the author may present information directly in what is called the *authorial voice*. Blatant cases of this are called "authorial intrusion." If the author comments at will on the characters and the action, serving as the all-knowing *narrator* throughout, the point of view is called "omniscient." This is rare in contemporary fiction. Many works combine the author's comments with sections strictly from a character's point of view in what is called "limited omniscience."

Melodrama,   72. Writing which is dominated by *conflict*, suspense, and a succession of *dramatic questions* at the expense of credible *characterization* and the subtle development of *theme*. It is simple writing (see *sophisticated fiction*) but has wide appeal. Subject matter includes war, spies, terrorism, horror, and the supernatural.

Metaphor and **simile,**   106ff. *Figures of speech* in which one item is compared with another which is different in all but a few significant respects. Similes make this comparison explicit with "like" or "as." Example: "She was like a tiger when fighting for equal rights." With metaphors, the comparison is implied: "She was a tiger when fighting for equal rights." The most common use of both metaphors and similes is to illustrate and dramatize abstract qualities.

Multitrack plot,   82. See *plot*.

Narrative modes,   24. Five methods by which *fiction* is presented: dialogue, thoughts, action, description, and exposition (direct analysis). Most fiction uses all five in varying ratios. Emphasizing any one will affect the *style* and *tone*. Example: Stressing action tends to make fiction "dramatic" and "dynamic" while concentrating on thoughts will make it "introspective" or, if well done, "penetrating." The modes are also the primary means of portraying *character*.

Narrative sequence,   84. See *plot*.

Narrative tension,   67. See *tension*.

Narrator,   49. The fictional *character* in a first-person work (see *person*) who appears to be relating the story. The narrator (sometimes called the "persona") may be an identified and named character or only an implied "speaker." When such a character gives information or opinions which later prove to be wrong, he or she is described as an "unreliable narrator." Narrators should not be confused with their authors.

Neutral style,   50. A manner of writing in which the *style* (diction, syntax, balance of *narrative modes*, and the like) is not noticeable or distinctive. Neutral style is contrasted with *as-if-spoken style*, "sparse style" (such as Hemingway's), or "formal style" (such as Henry James').

Nonchronological plot,   83. See *plot*.

Omniscient point of view,   55. See *means of perception*.

Outline,   129. A summary of the various points in a theme or essay written in the form of major and minor headings. In a "two-tier" outline, the major headings are usually identified with Roman numerals (I, II, III, . . .), and the subheadings with capital letters. Three- and four-tier outlines can be used for longer papers.

Parody,   104. See *satire*.

Person,   48. Essentially, the distinction between stories using "I" and those using "he" or "she." Technically, it is a grammatical distinction which identifies two types of fiction: that which is an illusion of an individual telling a story about him- or herself ("I had an adventure") and, on the other hand, fiction which is presented without even an implied narrator ("He had an adventure" or "She had an adventure"). Using "I" is the "first person" and "he" or "she" the "third person." Occasionally fiction is written in the second-person singular ("you"), the first-person plural ("we"), or the third person ("they"), but these forms are very rare. Person is *how* a story is presented; the *means of perception* is *who* appears to present it.

Persona,   49. See *narrator*.

Personification,   107. See *figure of speech*.

Picaresque novel,   83. A type of episodic novel (see *plot*) in which the *protagonist*, usually telling his or her own story in the first *person*, is a rogue and often a comic survivor of many somewhat unrelated aventures. *Moll Flanders* by Daniel Defoe is a good example.

Plot,   79. The sequence of events or *scenes* in a work of fiction. In a "chronological plot" the scenes are arranged in the same order as they occurred. A "nonchronological plot" shifts this order by including lengthy *flashbacks* or by using a *frame*. Nonchronological plots have a "factual sequence" (events as they happened) and a "narrative sequence" (the order in, which the author has presented them). The use of one or more subplots to echo or contrast with the primary story line is called a "multitrack plot." When the plot is a series of adventures which are not closely related, the work is called an "episodic novel."

Point of view,   52. See *means of perception*.

Private symbol,   110. See *symbol*.

Protagonist,   20. The primary *character* in a work of *fiction*. It is a broader term than "hero" or "heroine" since it includes both sexes and does not imply greatness or nobility. A character who opposes the protagonist is referred to as the "antagonist."

Public symbol,   110. See *symbol*.

Resolution,   70. See *tension*.

Rising action,   70. See *tension*.

Round character,   20. See *characterization*.

Satire,   104. A form of wit (see *comedy*) in which a distorted view of *characters*, places, or institutions is used for the purpose of criticism or ridicule. At least some measure of exaggeration (if only through a biased selection of details) is necessary. Satire is almost always presented with an *ironic tone*. When the characteristic *style* of an author or individual work is ridiculed by exaggeration, the result is called a "parody."

Scene, 79. A unit of action usually identified by place (the *setting*), by a particular *character* or group of characters, and occasionally by activity. Although some scenes are clearly designated, others are less precise. A "dramatic scene" in *fiction* refers to one in which action and *conflict* dominate.

Scope, 36. See *setting.*

Setting, 35ff. Most commonly, the geographic area in which a *fictional scene* or a fictional work as a whole takes place. The breadth or narrowness of this area is called the "scope." Panoramic novels like *War and Peace* have a wide scope; stories limited to a single room, like "A & P," have a narrow scope. Setting also includes the time of day, the season, the historical period ("temporal setting"), and the social milieu ("social setting").

Shock, 72. See *tension.*

Simile, 106. See *metaphor.*

Simple fiction, 1. See *sophisticated fiction.*

Social setting, 40. See *setting.*

Sophisticated fiction, 1. *Fiction* containing *characters* who are complex, situations which are unusual and have many ramifications, and *themes* which reveal subtle insights. Sophisticated fiction is at the opposite end of the scale from "simple fiction" in which the *characters* are often stereotypes or at least "flat" (one dimensional), the situations are familiar, and the themes conventional ("crime doesn't pay," "falling in love with the wrong person is a big mistake," and the like). "Sophisticated" and "simple" are descriptive terms, not value judgments. Those who enjoy sophisticated novels also turn off with "summer reading" from time to time.

Static characters, 20. See *characterization.*

Stereotype, 20. See *characterization.*

Stock characters, 20. See *characterization.*

Stream-of-consciousness writing, 51. *Fiction* in the form of a *character's* uninterrupted thoughts quoted without exposition, dialogue, or action. Such writing is essentially an unbroken interior monologue. The illusion is often created with run-on sentences and an apparently random sequence of ideas and impressions linked more by association than by logic. The technique is usually used, if at all, in individual *scenes* rather than as the basis of an entire novel.

Style, 96ff. The manner of expression which distinguishes one piece of writing from another. It is how a writer uses the language. Variations in style are created by choices in diction (word choice), *syntax* (sentence structure), and the differing emphasis on the five *narrative modes* (action, dialogue, thoughts, description, and exposition).

Subplot, 82. See *plot.*

Surprise, 71. See *tension.*

Suspense, 70. See *tension.*

Symbol, 109ff. Any detail—an object, action, or state—which has a range of meaning beyond and usually larger than its literal definition. The word *dove*, for example, refers to a type of bird (its "denotative meaning"), but it has also come to stand for those who favor arms reduction (its *connotative* or symbolic meaning). Symbols which are generally recognized by the public (like the dove, the hawk, spring) are "public symbols." Those devised by an author in a particular work or works are "private symbols."

Syntax, 98. Sentence structure. Types include "simple" (one subject and one verb), "compound" (two idea units or "clauses," each of which has a subject and a verb), and "complex" (an independent clause with one or more dependent clauses). A "periodic sentence" is one in which the full meaning is not completed until the end. Syntax (including the density and type of modifiers) is a major factor in establishing an author's *style*.

Temporal setting,   38. See *setting*.

Tension,   67. The dynamic quality in *fiction* frequently achieved through *conflict* but also created by means of *dramatic questions* (withholding information), suspense, surprise (a sudden release of information), and shock. Also called "narrative tension," this is the element which arouses the reader's curiosity and makes a work "dramatic." When the tension mounts, that portion of the *plot* is referred to as "rising action." The emotional high point or *climax* is often followed by a "resolution."

Theme,   116. The abstract suggestion or suggestions implied in a work of *fiction*. Also called "central concern." There are often several related themes ("multiple themes"), especially in novels. Sometimes they can be seen as "layered" in the sense that there are deeper suggestions beneath the initial and most obvious theme. Themes are usually subtle and implied rather than stated.

Thesis,   121. (1) In nonfiction the thesis is the central assertion of the paper. It is more specific than a "topic" and is usually described in the form of a complete sentence known as the "thesis statement." (2) In fiction the term refers to a clearly defined position or argument—usually religious or political. Most works of fiction, however, contain *themes* rather than theses.

Third-person fiction,   48, 52. See *person*.

Thoughts,   25. See *narrative modes*.

Time distortion,   86. *Fiction* which significantly distorts our notion of the normal flow of time. Although all fiction alters time by skipping over uneventful or unimportant periods, some works startle the reader by radical and unexpected distortions. These are not necessarily nonchronological *plots*. Usually a scene or scenes which we thought were of normal duration turn out to be imaginary (a dream, fantasy, hallucination, and the like). Examples: the dream in "On the Road" by Langston Hughes and the lengthy fantasy which occurs in a split second in "An Occurrence at Owl Creek Bridge" by Ambrose Bierce.

Tone,   101. The attitude an author or a *narrator* takes toward the material and toward his or her audience. Like tone of voice, literary tone is described as formal or informal, comic (see *comedy*) or serious, *ironic* or literal, *satiric* or "straight." In first-person works (see *person*), the *narrator* may appear to take the situation more seriously or more lightly than does the author. In such instances, the tone of the work as a whole is called ironic (see *irony*).

Topic,   126. See *thesis*.

Topic sentence,   132. The sentence which unifies a paragraph by stating the main idea. It is frequently placed at the beginning, but often it is implied rather than stated.

Unreliable narrator,   50. See *narrator*.

Utopian novel,   122. A novel which describes an ideal society. It is contrasted with the "antiutopian novel," which is set in a society which is terrible. Both types of *plots* tend to be didactic and are usually dominated by a strong *thesis*, sometimes at the expense of *characterization*.

Verbal irony,   103. See *irony*.

Wit,   102. See *comedy*.